THE
BIG SECRET
FOR THE
SMALL
INVESTOR

THE
BIG SECRET
FOR THE
SMALL
INVESTOR

A
New Route
to Long-Term
Investment
Success

JOEL GREENBLATT

CROWN
BUSINESS
NEW YORK

Copyright © 2011 by Joel Greenblatt

Published in the United States by Crown Business, an imprint of the Crown Publishing Group, a division of Random House, Inc., New York.

www.crownpublishing.com

CROWN BUSINESS is a trademark and CROWN and the Rising Sun colophon are registered trademarks of Random House, Inc.

Crown Business books are available at special discounts for bulk purchases for sales promotions or corporate use. Special editions, including personalized covers, excerpts of existing books, or books with corporate logos, can be created in large quantities for special needs. For more information, contact Premium Sales at (212) 572-2232 or e-mail specialmarkets@randomhouse.com.

Library of Congress Cataloging-in-Publication Data
Greenblatt, Joel.
    The big secret for the small investor : a new route to long-term investment success / Joel Greenblatt.—1st ed.
        p. cm.
    1. Investments.   2. Stocks.   3. Portfolio management.   I. Title.
HG4521.G696 2011
332.6—dc22

                                    2010051747

ISBN 978-0-385-52507-7
eISBN 978-0-307-72078-8

Printed in the United States of America

Book design by Gretchen Achilles

1 3 5 7 9 10 8 6 4 2

FIRST EDITION

To my wonderful wife, Julie,
and our five magnificent spinoffs.

CONTENTS

THE
BIG SECRET
FOR THE
SMALL
INVESTOR

INTRODUCTION

When it comes to investing in the stock market, investors have plenty of options:

1. They can do it themselves. Trillions of dollars are invested this way. (Of course, the only problem here is that most people have no idea how to analyze and choose individual stocks. Wait, did I say the only problem? I really meant most investors have no idea how to construct a stock portfolio, most have no idea when to buy and sell, and most have no idea how much to invest in the market in the first place. Okay, that's better.)

2. They can give it to professionals to invest. Trillions of dollars are invested this way. (Though, after fees and other institutional impediments, most don't add value. In fact, most professionals actually underperform the market averages over time. Oh, I almost forgot—it may be even harder

to pick good professional managers than it is to pick good individual stocks.)

3. They can invest in traditional index funds. Trillions of dollars are also invested this way. (This is a great way to match the major market averages, to pay very low fees, and to beat most professional managers. Then again, investing this way is seriously flawed—and almost a guarantee of subpar investment returns over time.)

4. They can read *The Big Secret for the Small Investor* and do something else. Not much is invested this way. (Yet . . .)

For years individual investors have asked me how they should go about investing their savings in the stock market. After all, I'm a longtime business school professor and institutional money manager, and they figure I should know. Yet for years I haven't had a good answer. You see, Wall Street isn't very kind to small investors. While it's true that individual investors have many options, for one reason or another (and usually one reason *and* another) most choices aren't very good. Well, with this book, I finally have what I think is a good answer to that very important question. And it's an answer that should work well for investors both big and small.

Then again, this is my third investing book. The first one, *You Can Be a Stock Market Genius* (yes, I know, I know), was meant to help the individual investor, too. It didn't. It assumed investors had a lot of specialized investment knowledge and a lot of free time. (Actually, it did end up helping a few dozen hedge fund managers, but . . .) My second book, *The Little Book That Beats the Market*, gave a step-by-step method for the individual investor to just "do it yourself." I still believe strongly in this method and I still love that book. But here, too, I missed the boat. As it turns out, most people don't want to do it themselves. Yes, they want to understand it. But they still want someone else to do it for them.

So maybe the third time really *is* the charm. *The Big Secret for the Small Investor* should be a great answer for many investors. I don't think most individual or even institutional investors have considered this solution for how best to invest in the stock market. I sincerely believe they should. In any case, I think both novice and sophisticated investors will benefit from the discussion. Good luck.

When I went to business school back in the late seventies (note to my kids: that's the 1970s!), we learned one important thing about stock market investing. It was simply this: there are so many smart people out there, *you* can't outsmart them. In other words, thousands of intelligent, knowledgeable people buy and sell stocks all day long, and as a result, stock prices reflect the collective judgment of all these smart people. If the price of a stock is too high, these smart people will sell until the price comes down to a lower, more reasonable price. If a stock price is too low, smart people will go in and buy until the stock's price rises to a fair level. This whole process happens so quickly, we were taught, that in general stock prices correctly reflect all currently available information. If, indeed, prices are accurate, there is no use in trying to "beat the market." In other words, according to my professors, the only way I was going to find a bargain-priced stock was by luck.

Naturally, I didn't listen (which, unfortunately, made this no different from most of my other classes).

But flash forward a few decades and now I'm the professor. Each year I teach a course in investing at a top Ivy League business school. The students are clearly smart, accomplished, and dedicated. In short, they are the best and the brightest. But every year for the last fourteen, I have walked into class on the very first day and told my students something eerily familiar and very disturbing. I tell them this: "Most of your peers and predecessors who learn about investing at business schools across the nation and beyond will go out into the real investing world and try to 'beat the market.' And almost all of them will do one thing in common—fail!"

How can this be? If brains and dedication aren't the deciding factors in determining who can be a successful investor, what are? If an Ivy League business school education doesn't determine investment success, what does? Are we really just back to where we started? After decades of investment experience and learning, were my business school professors right after all? The only way to beat the market is by luck?

Well, not exactly. I'm still glad I didn't listen to my professors. Investors *can* beat the market. It's just that becoming a successful investor doesn't have much to do with being one of the best and the brightest. It doesn't have much to do with attending a top business school (though being stupid with no degree isn't much help, either). Success also has nothing to do with an ability to master the economic and business news that bombards us each day. And success can't be found by following the hundreds of expert opinions offered on television, in newspapers, and in investment books. The secret to beating the market, as unlikely as it sounds, is in learning just a few simple concepts that almost anyone can master. These simple concepts serve as a road map, a road map that provides a way through all the noise, confusion, and bad directions. A road map that most smart MBAs, investment professionals, and amateur investors simply don't have.

And that makes sense. If being smart or having a business degree were all it took, there would be many thousands of individual and professional investors with great long-term investment records. There aren't. The answer, it seems clear, must lie elsewhere.

But that leaves us with another problem. If the answer is really as simple as I appear to be saying, in effect pretty much anyone can sign up to beat the market. How can that be? Why, if it's so simple, aren't there thousands of successful investors out there? This whole thing is starting not to make sense.

Well, the truth is it does make sense. The concepts needed to be a successful stock market investor *are* simple. Most people *can* do it. It's just that most people won't. Understanding why they won't (or don't) is the crucial first step to becoming a successful investor. Once we understand why most others fail, we can fully appreciate the simple solution.

But this understanding comes with a price. We need to start from the beginning and build our case step by step. Understanding where the value of a business comes from, how markets work, and what really happens on Wall Street will lead us to some important conclusions. It will also lead small investors (and even not-so-small investors) to some very good investment choices.

What I tell my students on the first day of class is still true. Most individuals, MBAs, and professionals who try to beat the market—won't. But you can. Let's see why.

was having a bad week. In no particular order: I dropped out of law school (understandably, my parents weren't too thrilled), broke up with my girlfriend (okay, she broke up with me, but at the time I had no idea that was actually a good thing), locked my keys in the car—twice (once in the ignition with the engine still running and once in the trunk at 11 p.m. after a Yankees game in the Bronx—and as you probably know, everybody's a 24-hour locksmith but no one really works those 24 hours all in a row), and finally, went through a toll booth with no money (after a few eye rolls and since Guantánamo was not yet taking prisoners, they let me mail it in, with the stamp costing more than the actual toll).

Luckily, the true value of a life cannot be summed up by a single bad week or even a series of bad months but by the total of everything we do and accomplish over a period of many years. I bring this up not to relive the glory days of my youth (such as they were) but because if you want to learn how to be a good investor, you're going to have to have a good understanding of the concept of "value"—what it is and where it comes from. This is pretty important because the secret to successful investing is fairly simple: first figure out the value of something—and then pay a lot less. I'll repeat that: **the secret to successful investing is to figure out the value of something—and then pay a lot less.**

Benjamin Graham, the acknowledged father of security analysis, called this "investing with a *margin of safety.*" The larger the space between current price and calculated value, the larger our margin of safety. Graham figured that if unexpected events lower the value of our purchase or our initial valuation is mistakenly high, buying with a large margin of safety will still protect us from big losses.

That's all fine, but what is "value" and where *does* it come from? The corner candy store might have a great location and a booming business, and at a price of $150,000 that business might be a great investment. But buy that same candy store for $50 million, same great location, same booming business, and you've pretty much guaranteed yourself a terrible investment (and created a whole mystery about how you got the $50 mil in the first place). In short, if we invest without understanding the value of what we're buying, we'll have little chance of making an intelligent investment.

In the same way that one lousy week didn't end up defining the value of my entire life, it turns out that the value of a business doesn't have that much to do with what happens each week or each month. Rather, the value of a business comes from how much that business can earn over its entire lifetime. That can often mean many years (and by many, I mean twenty, thirty, or even more—we can't just be thinking about earnings over the next two or three). While figuring out the earnings of a business over the next thirty-plus years might sound like a pretty hard thing to do, we're going to try to do it anyway. We'll start with a simple example, and by chapter's end, we should have a pretty good understanding of how this whole value thing is supposed to work. (And once we start to understand value, there's no telling what we can accomplish in the rest of the book!)

We'll even assume for the purposes of our simple example that we know (somehow) ahead of time what the earnings of our business will be over the next thirty years and beyond. To make it even simpler, we'll assume that the business in question, Candy's Candies, will earn $10,000 each year for the next thirty-plus years. So let's see what happens.

Intuitively, we know that collecting $10,000 each year for the next thirty years is not the same as receiving all $300,000 today. If we had that $300,000 right now, one easy thing we could do is to put it in the bank and then earn some interest on our deposit. The bank could take our money, pay us a few percent each year in interest, and then lend that money out to other people or businesses and collect a higher interest rate than they pay us. Everybody wins. By the time thirty years go by, we'd have a lot more than the original $300,000 from all the interest we collected. But, of course, Candy's Candies only earns $10,000 each year, and we'll have to wait thirty years to collect all $300,000. So let's break it down and see what thirty-plus years of earning $10,000 per year are really worth to us today.[1]

Let's assume for the sake of simplicity that we are the proud owners of Candy's Candies, that we collect all of our earnings at the end of each year, and that a bank will pay us 6 percent each year on any deposits that we make. So let's start by figuring out the value

---

1. These concepts involve a discussion of the *time value of money* and *discounted cash flow.* If you are already very familiar with these (and can't possibly see how I can make them funny), feel free to look at the pretty pictures and then skip ahead to the chapter summary!

today of collecting that first $10,000 in profits from our new business at the end of the first year and then we'll go from there.

We know that collecting $10,000 a year from now is not the same as having that $10,000 today. If we had the $10,000 right now, we could put it in the bank and earn 6 percent interest. At the end of the first year, we'd have $10,600, not merely $10,000. So the $10,000 we collect a year from now is worth less than $10,000 in our hands today. How much less? Pretty much the 6 percent less that we didn't get to earn in interest. The math looks like this: $10,000 one year from now discounted by the 6 percent we didn't get to earn is $10,000 ÷ 1.06, which equals $9,434. (Another way to look at it: if you had $9,434 today and deposited it in the bank at 6 percent, you would have $10,000 at the end of one year.)

So the value of our first year's earnings from Candy's Candies is worth $9,434 to us in today's dollars. How about the second year's earnings? What are those worth to us in today's dollars? Well, two years from now, we will be collecting another $10,000 in profits from our ownership of our candy business. What is $10,000 that we won't receive for two years worth today? Well, it works out to $8,900 ($10,000 ÷ 1.06^2). If we had $8,900 today and deposited it in the bank at 6 percent, we would have $10,000 by the end of the second year. And so the value today of our first two years of earnings from Candy's Candies is $9,434 + $8,900, or $18,334. (This is getting really exciting!)

I won't go through the next twenty-eight-plus years, but the exercise looks something like this:

VALUE OF CANDY'S CANDIES

YEAR 1		YEAR 2		YEAR 3		YEAR 4		YEAR 5
$\dfrac{\$10{,}000}{1.06}$	+	$\dfrac{\$10{,}000}{1.06^2}$	+	$\dfrac{\$10{,}000}{1.06^3}$	+	$\dfrac{\$10{,}000}{1.06^4}$	+	$\dfrac{\$10{,}000}{1.06^5}$
$9,434	+	8,900	+	$8,396	+	$7,921	+	$7,473

	YEAR 30		YEAR 31	
...	$\dfrac{\$10{,}000}{1.06^{30}}$	+	$\dfrac{\$10{,}000}{1.06^{31}}$	, etc. = $\boxed{\$166{,}667}$
	$1,741	+	$1,643	

$$* \text{Present Value} = \frac{\text{Annual Cash Flow}}{\text{Discount Rate}} = PV = \frac{c}{d} = \frac{\$10{,}000}{0.06} = \$166{,}667$$

So earning $10,000 a year for the next thirty-plus years turns out to be worth about $166,667 today. Using these simple assumptions, we just figured out something incredibly important. Candy's Candies, a business guaranteed to earn us $10,000 each year for the next thirty-plus years or so, is worth the same as having $166,667 cash in our pocket today! Now, here's the hard part. If we could be guaranteed that all of our assumptions were correct and someone offered to sell us Candy's Candies for $80,000, should we do it?

Well, here's another way to ask the same question. If someone offered to give us $166,667 right now in exchange for $80,000, should we do it? Given all of our assumptions, the answer is easy: of course we should do it! This is an incredibly important concept. If we can really figure out the value of a business like Candy's Candies, investing becomes very simple! Remember, **the secret to successful investing is to figure out the value of something and then—pay a lot less!** In fact, it couldn't be simpler: $166,667 is a lot more than $80,000—case closed.

Of course, there's one little problem. I made the "figuring out the value of something" part a bit too easy. How? Let me count the ways.

Remember, I told you ahead of time what the earnings of Candy's Candies were going to be each year for the next thirty-plus years. But will earnings actually shrink over those years? Will they grow? Will Candy's Candies even be around in another thirty years? In practice, predicting so far into the future is pretty hard to do. In addition, many businesses are actually more complicated than the corner candy store. In fact, forget thirty years—it turns out that Wall Street analysts are actually pretty bad at predicting earnings for even the next quarter or the next year. Are you really going to trust my predictions about what earnings will be over the next thirty years? (Remember, I can't remember the keys or the toll money, and I'm not even a lawyer!)

So here's the problem. Since no one really knows for sure what earnings will be over the next thirty-plus years, whatever we use for estimated earnings during that time is just going to be a guess. Even if this guess is made by a very smart, informed "expert," it will still be a guess. There will always be a chance that this guess is off, sometimes by a lot. So when we figure out the value of our business, we're going to have to assume that there is risk to our estimate of earnings for that business. The amount of earnings we expect to receive from owning that business over the next thirty-plus years will almost always be uncertain. Obviously, we'll make our best guess about what those earnings will be. But those earnings will always be far from a sure thing.

So here's the question. What would you pay more for—a guaranteed $10,000 a year for the next thirty-plus years, or a best guess of collecting $10,000 a year for the next thirty-plus years? It's pretty clear that a guarantee is worth more than a guess. In practice, investors discount the price they will pay for future earnings that are based only on estimates. If there is no guarantee that you will actually collect that $10,000 after the first year of owning Candy's Candies, you will probably pay less for those earnings than if they were guaranteed. In our simple example where next year's earnings of $10,000 were guaranteed, we discounted that payment by 6 percent, reflecting the fact that we had to wait a year to collect our $10,000. Now, with only an *estimated* $10,000 coming in at the end of the first year, we will pay less.

How much less? That's not exactly clear, but we would certainly discount that hoped-for $10,000 by more than the 6 percent we used when the $10,000 was guaranteed—maybe we'd use a discount of 8 percent or 10 percent or 12 percent, or even more (the amount of our discount would reflect in part how confident we were in our earnings estimate). But when we apply that higher discount to the next thirty-plus years of earnings estimates, that's when things really start to get silly (yes, it's true, math *can* be hilarious).

Here's what happens:

VALUE OF CANDY'S CANDIES

AT:	6% DISCOUNT RATE	8% DISCOUNT RATE	12% DISCOUNT RATE
	$\dfrac{\$10{,}000}{0.06} = \$166{,}667$	$\dfrac{\$10{,}000}{0.08} = \$125{,}000$	$\dfrac{\$10{,}000}{0.12} = \$83{,}333$

As it turns out, using a 12 percent discount rate, the value of Candy's Candies is only $83,333. We're starting to get in trouble! It's no longer so obvious that a purchase price of $80,000 is such a bargain!

What *is* crystal clear, however, is that using different discount rates for our estimated earnings can lead to wildly different results when we try to value a business. But figuring out the right discount rate isn't our only problem. For the sake of simplicity, we've made some other assumptions that don't really hold up in the real world. For instance, as you might intuitively guess, most companies don't earn the same amount each year for thirty straight years. As we've already touched on, many businesses grow their earnings over time, while others, due to competition, a bad product, or a poor business plan, see their earnings shrink or even disappear over the years. Let's see how funny the math gets when we try to value a business using not only different estimates for discount rates but we throw on top of that some different guesses for future earnings growth rates!

VALUE OF CANDY'S CANDIES

AT:	4% GROWTH RATE 8% DISCOUNT RATE	4% GROWTH RATE 12% DISCOUNT RATE	6% GROWTH RATE 8% DISCOUNT RATE
	$250,000	$125,000	$500,000
	$10,000	$10,000	$10,000
	————————	————————	————————
	(.08 −.04)	(.12 −.04)	(.08 −.06)

$$\frac{\text{Annual Cash Flow}}{\text{Discount Rate−Growth Rates}} = \text{Present Value}$$

Wow!!!! In other words, the math shows us something very important. According to finance theory and logic, the value of a business should equal the sum of all of the earnings that we expect to collect from that business over its lifetime[2] (discounted back to a value in today's dollars based upon how long it will take us to collect those earnings and how risky we believe

---

2. In reality, we should look for how much cash we receive from the business over its lifetime. For our purposes, we will assume that earnings are a good approximation for cash received.

our estimates of future earnings to be). Will earnings grow at 2 percent, 4 percent, 6 percent, or not at all? Is the right discount rate 8 percent, 10 percent, 12 percent, or some other number? The math says that small changes in estimated growth rates or discount rates or both can end up making huge differences in what value we come up with!

VALUE OF CANDY'S CANDIES

AT:	2% GROWTH RATE 12% DISCOUNT RATE	5% GROWTH 8% DISCOUNT RATE
	$100,000	$333,333
	$\dfrac{\$10,000}{(.12-.02)}$	$\dfrac{\$10,000}{(.08-.05)}$

$$\frac{\text{Annual Cash Flow}}{\text{Discount Rate–Growth Rates}} = \text{Present Value}$$

Which numbers are right? It's incredibly hard to know. Whose estimates of earnings over the next thirty-plus years should we trust? What discount rate is the right one to use?

So like I said, the secret to successful investing is to **figure out the value of something and then—pay a lot less!**

But how are we going to figure out value? How can anyone?

Good questions, but just because we can't answer them yet, we've learned some very valuable lessons anyway. So let's go to the summary and see what they are.

SUMMARY

1. The secret to successful investing is to figure out the value of something and then pay a lot less! (Thought I'd mention that!)

2. The value of a business is equal to the sum of all of the earnings we expect to collect from that business over its lifetime (discounted back to a value in today's dollars). Earnings over the next twenty or thirty years are where most of this value comes from. Earnings from next quarter or next year represent only a tiny portion of this value.

3. The calculation of value in #2 above is based on guesses. Small changes in our guesses about future earnings over the next thirty-plus years will result in wildly different estimates of value

for our business. Small changes in our guesses about the proper rate to discount those earnings back into today's dollars will also result in wildly different estimates of value for our business. Small changes in both will drive us crazy.

4. If our estimate of value can change dramatically with even small changes in our guesses about the proper earnings growth rate to use or the proper discount rate, how meaningful can the estimates of value made by "experts" really be?

5. The answer to #4 above is—"not very."

6. As it turns out, there actually are 24-hour locksmiths in the Bronx—unfortunately, they are not available now.

THREE

E very morning on my way to work, I am confronted by an inspiring message from, of all places, the U.S. Postal Service. Right there, on Eighth Avenue and Thirty-third Street, in New York City across from the train station, stands the majestic General Post Office building. Emblazoned across an entire city block on the front of the building is the well-known motto "Neither snow nor rain nor heat nor gloom of night stays these couriers from the swift completion of their appointed rounds." Yes, perhaps the mail used to be more important before texting, email, and the Internet took over our lives, but the nobility of the sentiment remains, coming through loud and clear: throw what obstacles you like in our way, it proclaims, we will fulfill our duty, complete our task, get the job done, and do it quickly to boot—no matter what. Come on, how great is that?

Of course, during a recent snowstorm it turns out

that it's "only a poem," according to our local post-
master.[1] But I still love the ideal of never giving up
no matter how difficult the task. So I don't really care
that we have no idea what earnings will be for the
next thirty-plus years for the businesses we are trying to value. I care even less that we don't know what
interest rate to use to discount those more than
thirty years of earnings. There just have to be other
ways to figure out the value of a company—and luckily for us, there are.

One of them is even pretty obvious. When you go to
buy a house, for example, everyone pretty much knows
to check around the neighborhood before doing any-
thing else. What does an average house in the same
neighborhood cost? Have there been any recent house
sales on my block? What were the sale prices? How does
the house I'm thinking about buying compare to the
other houses on the block, to the other houses in the
neighborhood, to similar houses in neighboring towns?
We all know the drill. These are simple and obvious
questions to ask and things to check out before we buy.

Well, it's pretty much the same with valuing companies. This method is often referred to as looking at

---

1. Actually, it's a poem written by a famous Greek historian 2,500 years
ago (but only delivered in the last few centuries, due to some unforeseen
weather conditions).

relative value. What business is the company in? How much are companies in similar businesses selling for? What is the relationship of the company's earnings to its price? Does that make it appear cheaper or more expensive than similar companies? What are the company's growth prospects? Are they better or worse than other companies in the same industry? Is that reflected in the price? There are all kinds of questions to ask and things to compare. Of course, this process isn't that simple, but having other similar companies and businesses to compare prices with is one of the methods investors use to keep from spending $50 million for the local candy store (obviously, not having $50 million is another effective way).

Looking at relative value makes complete sense and is an important and useful way to help value businesses. Unfortunately, there are times when this method doesn't work very well. We can all remember the Internet bubble of the late 1990s, when almost any company associated with the Internet (or even companies that knew a company associated with the Internet) traded at incredibly high and ultimately unjustifiable prices. Comparing one Internet company to another wasn't very helpful. Almost all Internet companies were incredibly overpriced during that time. We also know what happened in the recent real estate bubble.

Many houses appeared reasonably priced relative to other houses in the neighborhood. In reality, the whole neighborhood was vastly overpriced due to the easy availability of bank financing.

In the stock market this kind of relative mispricing happens all the time. An entire industry, like oil or construction, may be in favor because prospects look particularly good over the near term. A company in one of those industries may appear reasonably or even cheaply priced relative to other companies in the same industry. Yet when an entire industry is mispriced, even the cheapest oil company or the least expensive construction company may be massively overpriced! That's why it is very dangerous to rely on a relative value analysis alone when determining the value of a company.

So if valuing the next thirty-plus years of earnings can give us wildly different results with only slight changes in our assumptions, and looking at relative value can prove unreliable at the worst possible times, are there any other weapons left in the arsenal that investors can use to figure out the value of a company? Well, yes, sort of.

But, unfortunately, they're not that great, either. One of them involves figuring out what a company could be worth to someone else. This is commonly referred to as *acquisition value*. A good example of this has taken place in the online stock brokerage business. If you have two companies, one with 50,000 customers and one with 200,000 customers, it may pay for the larger company to buy the smaller one. Why? The larger company needs only one back office, one computer system, one chief executive, and so on. So what usually happens once a buyout takes place is that the smaller company's back office, computer system, and chief executive are no longer needed. The larger company can earn a lot more from the additional 50,000 customers than the smaller one can because it doesn't have to pay all the expenses of operating an independent company.

In fact, because of the cost savings of combining companies, sometimes the smaller company is worth more to the acquiring company than the value it would have if it continued to operate on its own. How do you figure out how much more? Who gets the benefit of the cost savings, the buying company or the selling company? Will management ever want to sell out regardless of how much value a sale of the business would generate? These questions need to be answered given the circumstances of each case, and while it's certainly possible to make some good guesses, it's not a simple process. But acquisition value, what a company may be worth to someone else, is an additional method investors should consider when trying to figure out the value of a company.

Still another valuation method is sometimes referred to as *liquidation value*. Here we look to the assets of the company, not just its earnings. Some companies are actually worth more "dead than alive." A company that loses money, for example, may be able to sell off its inventory, land, buildings, and even its brand names (if it has any) for more than the company would be worth if it continued to operate. (In one extreme example, a struggling owner of a horse racing track actually realized value from its assets by striking oil in the parking lot!) In most instances, however, an investor would have to determine how likely it would be for the management of the poorly performing company to close up shop and sell off all its assets. In practice, few managers of even money-losing companies voluntarily choose to eliminate their own jobs. Nevertheless, estimating the liquidation value of a company can be helpful in evaluating whether a company is available at a bargain price or not.

So of the four different methods that professional analysts use to figure out the value of a company, none is that easy to implement, and all present varying degrees of difficulty. To complicate things a bit further, in the real world many large companies are not merely in one business. Often larger companies have a number of different divisions, with each division in a different line of business or different industry from the others. Analysts may value one of the divisions by using some combination of discounted future earnings and relative value, and value other divisions using acquisition or liquidation value. This kind of analysis is usually called a *sum-of-the-parts valuation*, and it is just a logical way of adding up the results from a combination of best guesses and estimates using a mixture of the four methods just discussed.

By now, you're probably getting the point: It's not so easy to figure out the value of a company. If intelligent investing involves figuring out the value of something and then paying a lot less, this would probably be a good time to start questioning whether it's really worth finishing the book. Predicting earnings for the next thirty years sounds like a ridiculously hard thing to do. Figuring out what interest rate to use to discount those earnings? Just as hard! On the other hand, the relative value strategy makes a lot of sense and in some ways is actually much easier to do than the others. Then again, there aren't always similar companies to use for comparisons and even when there are, this method can often lead to the wrong answer at absolutely the worst time!

Figuring out acquisition value might have some promise. But this method requires us to have the ability to understand the economics of two businesses—the unknown potential buyer's and the company we are trying to value. Once we've mastered that, we'd have to do a cost-saving analysis for a business combination between the two companies. Then we would still have to assess how much of those potential savings would go to the selling company's owners rather than to the buyer. Anyway, best of luck with this one.

But at least we'll always be able to fall back on our liquidation value analysis. Just kidding! Almost no one liquidates. Why? In most cases, when things aren't going so well for a business, management acts just like the post office (or more accurately, the poem on the post office building)—rather than give up on the business or their jobs, they keep trying! If plan A doesn't work, don't worry, there's always plans B, C, D, and Z. A company's money and resources usually run out well before management runs out of new turnaround plans.

So where are we really? For one, we're at the end of Chapter 3 and you still don't know how to value a company. But you perhaps have learned something even more important. You now understand some of the challenges faced by professional analysts and money managers when *they* try to value a company. That's very valuable information. I'll try to explain how I attempt to meet some of these challenges in the next chapter, but for now, don't worry—you're actually doing great (even if you don't think so)!

SUMMARY

1. Figuring out how to value the next thirty-plus years of estimated earnings for a company isn't the only method investors can use to value a company.

2. Other methods, such as relative value, acquisition value, liquidation value, and something called sum-of-the-parts, can also be used to help calculate a fair value.

3. Unfortunately, all of these methods are difficult to use and can often lead to seriously inaccurate estimates of value.

4. Once again, if we don't know how to value a business, we can't invest in it intelligently.

5. The post office can't really help us (it's snowing or raining or very dark out or something), but I'll do what I can in the next chapter.

So I'm taking the final exam for a course on Shakespeare and I'm starting to sweat. My predicament is entirely my own fault. I'm at an undergraduate business school, after all, and no one forced me to sign up for a class on the works of a sixteenth-century playwright. It's just that for some reason I stopped by the first lecture and there was a visiting professor from England reading the powerful opening lines from *Richard III* with this great British accent. Genuinely smitten, I signed up for the course on the spot. Luckily, in a moment of what historians will no doubt record as sheer genius, I checked off the box to take the class pass/fail. Admittedly, I could have worked harder during the semester (by actually reading all the plays instead of just *CliffsNotes*), but there I was sitting in the final exam living in real life the recurring nightmare that most every student and adult has had at some point. But this wasn't a dream and I didn't know any of the answers.

No, really. It wasn't even a close call. Twelve lines from any of I-don't-know-how-many plays we were supposed to have read. Who said it? Which play and what scene? What was the context and significance? That was the whole exam. What the hell was I supposed to do? Frankly, I did know the guy sitting next to me, but to put it politely, he was a complete idiot, so that wasn't an option. With literally nowhere to turn, I sweated through my shirt and my undershorts in the middle of December and proceeded to put down twelve clearly wrong answers (unless Polonius really did advise Romeo to just "go for it!").

But here's the thing: I passed. As it turned out, almost everyone found the exam impossible. Combined with probably the most generous curve of all time, it really helped that so many other students were in the same predicament. So keep this story in mind as I share with you how I try to deal with all the problems involved in trying to value a company. Yes, all the difficult issues that we've already discussed will still be there. But always remember that everyone else has to deal with these same issues also. Under the right circumstances, your guesses will likely be just as good, and sometimes even better, than those of many "experts." The significance of this state of affairs will be examined a bit later, but before we get there, let's see if we can learn a few tricks of the trade.

We'll begin by tackling the toughest problem of all. How in the world do we go about estimating the next thirty-plus years of earnings and, on top of that, try to figure out what those earnings are worth today? The answer is actually simple: we don't. Instead, we just make the challenge easier.

We start with the assumption that there are other alternatives for our money. In my book, the main competition that any investment has to beat is how much we could earn "risk-free" by loaning money to the U.S. government. For our example (and for some reasons I'll discuss later), we'll assume that we could buy a ten-year U.S. Treasury bond that will pay us 6 percent a year for ten years. This is essentially lending the U.S. government money for those ten years with a guarantee that they will pay us 6 percent each year and then pay us all of our money back at the end of that time.

Now we finally have a simple standard that we can use to compare all of our other investment choices. If we don't expect an investment will beat the 6 percent per year that is available risk-free from the U.S. government, then we won't invest. That's a great start! Let's see what happens when we use our new tool to evaluate an investment in Candy's Candies.

If you remember Candy's Candies from Chapter 2, it's really just our neighborhood candy shop. The business is for sale at a price of $100,000. Our best guess is that the business will earn $10,000 after taxes next year[1] and that earnings will continue to grow a little bit each year as the town continues to expand. So here's the question. If we invest $100,000 to buy the entire Candy's Candies business and we earn $10,000 on our investment next year, is that better than taking that same $100,000 and investing in a U.S. government bond paying a guaranteed 6 percent per year for the next ten years? Let's see.

The most obvious thing we can say right off the bat is that earning $10,000 in the first year on an investment of $100,000 is equal to a 10 percent return on our money $(10,000 \div 100,000 = 10\%)$. This is usually referred to as an *earnings yield* of 10 percent. That's certainly higher than the 6 percent risk-free return we can get by lending money to the U.S. government. But, unfortunately, that's not the end of the analysis. The 6

---

1. In practice, I assume that next year will be a "normal" year for the business. A "normal" year is one where the economic and business conditions are typical, not extraordinarily good or bad.

percent from the government is guaranteed, while the 10 percent from Candy's Candies is just our best guess. Also, the 6 percent is guaranteed for ten years. The 10 percent return is our best guess for only next year's earnings. On the other hand, in future years we expect that 10 percent return to grow as earnings increase each year. In short, we are comparing a guaranteed 6 percent annual return that doesn't grow or shrink to an expected but risky 10 percent return that we think will grow each year (but since it's a guess, it could also shrink or disappear completely). How do we compare the two investments?

Here's where it gets interesting. Are we very confident of our earnings estimate for Candy's Candies? Are we very confident that earnings will grow over time? Of course, if we are, a 10 percent return that grows even larger as each year goes by could well be very attractive when compared to a flat 6 percent return. If we're not very confident about our estimates, we might determine that the sure 6 percent from the government is a better deal. But that's not all we can do with this analysis. Now, we also have a way to compare an investment in Candy's Candies with some of our other investment opportunities.

Let's say we also have a chance to buy our local Bad Bob's Barbeque Restaurant. Bad Bob's is also available for $100,000 (Bad Bob and batteries not included). We expect Bad Bob's will earn $12,000 next year. That's a 12 percent earnings yield for the first year. We also expect that earnings will grow even faster than Candy's Candies over time. In addition, we are more confident in our estimates for earnings and future growth prospects for Bad Bob's than we are for Candy's Candies. So while we still don't know if either investment is more attractive than a government bond, we at least know that we think Bad Bob's is a more attractive investment than Candy's Candies. Why? This one's easy. We expect to earn a 12 percent first-year return on our investment in Bad Bob's versus 10 percent for Candy's Candies, we expect that 12 percent return to grow faster than Candy's Candies, and we have more confidence in our estimates for the local barbeque place than we do for the candy store.

So first we compare a potential investment against what we could earn risk-free with our money (for purposes of our discussion and for reasons that will be detailed later, we have set the minimum risk-free rate that we will have to beat at a 6 percent annual return). If we have high confidence in our estimates and our investment appears to offer a significantly higher annual return over the long term than the risk-free rate, we've passed the first hurdle. Next, we compare our potential investment with our other investment alternatives. In our example, Bad Bob's offers a higher expected annual return and a higher growth rate, and we are even more confident in our estimates than we are for Candy's Candies. So we obviously prefer Bad Bob's over Candy's Candies. Of course, if we have high confidence that both investment alternatives offer a better deal than the risk-free government bond, we can always decide to buy both. But, in general, this is the basic process that I go through when evaluating and comparing businesses to invest in for my own portfolio.

When I teach this concept to my MBA students, at this point in the discussion I always ask them the following questions: What happens if we are trying to value a company and we're having a hard time estimating future earnings and growth rates? What if the industry is very competitive and we're just not sure if current earnings are sustainable? Maybe we have a question about whether some of their new products will be successful. Sometimes we're not sure how new technologies will affect a company's main service or product. What are we supposed to do then?

My answer is always simple: skip that company and find one that's easier to evaluate. If you don't have a good idea about what's going to happen in the industry, with the company's new products or services, or the effects of new technology on the company, then you can't really make good estimates for future earnings or growth rates. If you can't do that, you have no business investing in that company in the first place!

But I know what you're thinking: *Thanks for the advice, but this stuff still sounds really hard to do.*

In reality, I don't expect even my best MBA students to be very good at making estimates of future earnings and growth rates for most companies. In fact, I tell them not to bother. In the stock market, no one forces you to invest. You have thousands of companies to choose from. I tell them the best course of action is to find the few companies where you have a good understanding of the business, the industry, and the future prospects for earnings. Then make your best estimates and comparisons for the handful of companies you *can* evaluate. For these companies, an evaluation can also include relative value analysis, acquisition value analysis, or some of the other methods that we've already discussed.

But that's what I tell *them*. What I'll tell you is that you're absolutely right: this stuff *is* hard. But that was my point all along. All that I want is for you to begin to understand some of the challenges faced by professional investment managers. I want you to appreciate how tough it must be to make confident estimates for dozens and sometimes hundreds of companies. I want you to understand the questions that need to be asked, the comparisons that need to be made, and the complicated assessments that have to be reached about the future.

In fact, these issues are so tough, it's kind of like we're all stuck taking that Shakespeare final together! But don't worry yet. If Hamlet can make it, so can we. (Wait, did Hamlet make it?) Anyway, there's plenty more ahead—including a discussion about all the things I tell my students to do, an examination of what most professional investment managers actually do, and finally, advice for what most of you should do (hint: it doesn't involve making a single estimate!).

But first, let's go to the summary and review what we've learned so far.

SUMMARY

1. It's hard to make earnings estimates for the next thirty-plus years. It's hard to figure out what those earnings are worth today. So we don't.

2. Instead, when we evaluate the purchase price of a company, we make sure that our investment

will return more than the 6 percent per year we could earn risk-free from the U.S. government (see the box on page 53 for further explanation).

3. If our investment appears to offer a significantly higher annual return over the long term than the risk-free rate and we have high confidence in our estimates, we've passed the first hurdle.

4. Next, we compare the expected annual returns of our potential investment and our level of confidence in those returns to our other investment alternatives.

5. If we can't make a good estimate of the future earnings for a particular company, we skip that one and find a company we *can* evaluate.

6. It's really hard for investment professionals to make estimates and comparisons for dozens and sometimes hundreds of companies.

7. We're about to learn what I tell my students to do so that they can meet some of these challenges.

8. If Hamlet can make it, so can we! (Unfortunately, I just checked and it turns out Hamlet is a tragedy.)

Why is 6 percent the minimum annual return that any investment should beat? Why do we look at the ten-year U.S. Treasury bond? What if the ten-year Treasury bond is paying less than 6 percent? What if the ten-year bond is paying more than 6 percent?

Obviously, if we can earn 6 percent per year on our investments without taking any risk, we should invest in something else only if we have confidence that that investment will pay us a much higher rate over the long term. The ten-year U.S. government bond, though not perfect, is the closest we can come to a guarantee of a risk-free fixed interest rate and the return of all of our initial investment.

Although the risk-free U.S. government bond rate is sometimes less than 6 percent, we use 6 percent as our minimum to be conservative.[2] We look at the ten-year bond because ten years is a relatively long time (using a thirty-year bond rate would also be acceptable).

If the ten-year bond rate is above 6 percent, we would use that higher number. Obviously, if we could earn 8

---

2. In other words, using 6 percent as a minimum threshold to beat, regardless of how low government rates go, should give us added confidence that we are making a good long-term investment. (This should protect us if very low government bond rates are not a permanent condition.)

percent risk-free, that would be the rate our other investments should have to beat.

What if we find a company for $100,000 that we expect to earn only $5,000 next year? Could we ever buy that company, since that would only give us a 5 percent annual return? The answer is actually yes. If we had high confidence that in a few years that company's earnings would grow so much that it would be earning $10,000 or $12,000 per year, we might consider it. In other words, the company would soon be returning 10 percent or 12 percent per year even though next year it would only be returning 5 percent. Under these circumstances, it could be better than our risk-free return.

This stuff is hard. Let's see if the next chapter helps a little.

CHAPTER

FIVE

So here's a question: What strategy would you use to beat Tiger Woods? After all, he's already won fourteen major championships. Even other professionals have a tough time trying to beat him. How could a hacker like you ever hope to win? Well, it turns out you have a much better chance than you think. Just don't play him in golf!

When it comes to the stock market, that's the kind of advice I give to my students (oh, quiet, I'm making a point here). Many professional investment managers run billions of dollars. They have large, experienced staffs, access to new talent from top business schools, extensive resources, and research help from all the major Wall Street firms. Many of these same managers are also very smart. When they analyze dozens or even hundreds of companies, most are trying to figure out all the same things we've already talked about: What will future earnings be? How fast will earnings grow? How much confidence do we have in our predictions?

How do I tell my students to compete with all those smart guys with all that money and all those resources? It's simple, really. I just tell them to play a different game. In fact, some of the greatest battles in history have been won by armies that are severely outmanned and outgunned. If your side has ten thousand troops and you're up against an enemy with a hundred thousand, intuitively it doesn't make much sense to run right at them (even if you go in yelling and screaming). The enemy would love that! To win, you have to pick your spots, sneak up on them, sneak around them, bluff them, cut off their supplies, or wait them out. Whatever the strategy, a head-on battle is probably the wrong way to go! To put the odds in your favor, you have to change the game.

As it turns out, when it comes to the stock market, there are a number of ways to do just that. One of the best is to fly a little below the radar, to buy shares in smaller companies where the big boys simply can't play.

Despite how it appears in the newspapers or on television, the basics of the stock market aren't all that complicated. A share of stock represents an ownership interest in a company. Those ownership interests are divided into shares. If a company divides its ownership into one million shares, each share represents a one-millionth ownership interest in the entire company. These shares trade each day in an electronic marketplace that we know as the stock market. If you are able to buy one hundred thousand of the one million shares (referred to as one million shares *outstanding*), you can own 10 percent of the company. That 10 percent stake at $10 per share would cost you $1 million. A price of $10 per share for a company with a total of one million shares outstanding would mean that the stock market is valuing the entire company at $10 million ($10 per share $\times$ 1 million shares).

But a company that the market values at a total of only $10 million (known as a *market capitalization* of $10 million) is much too small for almost all institutional investors (mutual funds, pension funds, endowments, insurance companies, etc.) to buy. Even companies with market capitalizations in the hundreds of millions are often too small for these types of institutions to own. Most institutional investors, for legal and other reasons, must limit their ownership stakes to 5 or 10 percent of the total company. Purchasing even 5 percent of a company's shares can often push the purchase price up, particularly for very small companies whose shares do not trade very much. It's generally not worth it for institutions with hundreds of millions or billions to invest to bother with individual companies with market capitalizations below $500 million or even $1 billion. They just can't buy enough of these smaller companies to make it worth doing the work. Most research analysts from Wall Street firms won't usually cover these smaller companies, either. The companies' shares don't trade enough to generate enough commissions to justify the cost of the research coverage.

But there are thousands of companies that trade in the United States with market capitalizations below $1 billion. There are thousands more international companies that trade in developed markets around the world and have market capitalizations below $1 billion. So investing in smaller-capitalization stocks is a game involving thousands of companies worldwide, and most institutions are just too big to play. Luckily, you're not. At least, that's what I tell my students.

Of course, you still have to make guesses and estimates to figure out what these companies are worth. It's just better to have less competition from the big boys when searching for bargain-priced companies. It's also better to have thousands more companies to choose from when making investing decisions (individuals can choose from both large- *and* small-cap stocks). So having a small amount of money (even millions or tens of millions is considered small for these purposes) is a big advantage in the investment world. Less competition and more choices are a real advantage. As Warren Buffett has pointed out, "A fat wallet is the enemy of high investment returns." What he means is that as his wealth has grown, his investment options have narrowed. There are now only a relatively few investment opportunities that are large enough to make a difference to the overall investment returns of his portfolio. His choices are generally limited to well-known companies, where he must compete with thousands of large institutional investors to find investment bargains.

So not having billions of dollars to invest is a great way to gain an edge over the big Wall Street firms. But, assuming my students can check that box off, are there other ways they can change the game? Well, there is another strategy that they all seem to like. It involves being a little lazy. I tell them not to try to analyze hundreds of companies. It's really hard to have a high degree of confidence in predicting future earnings for more than a handful of companies, anyway. But it is possible, and certainly much easier, to find six or ten companies over time where you have a high degree of confidence in the prospects for future earnings, growth rates, and new industry developments.

It just seems logical that sticking to investing in only a small number of companies that you understand well, rather than moving down the list to your thirtieth or fiftieth favorite pick, would create a much greater potential to earn above-average investment returns. John Maynard Keynes, the well-known British economist, famously put it this way: "As time goes on, I get more and more convinced that the right method of investment is to put fairly large sums into enterprises which one thinks one knows something about and in the management of which one thoroughly believes." According to Buffett, "We believe that a policy of portfolio concentration may well decrease risk if it raises, as it should, both the intensity with which an investor thinks about a business and the comfort level he must feel with its economic characteristics before buying into it."

Sticking to analyzing and investing in a few companies where you have special insight or some deeper knowledge makes good sense. I know a number of investors who have even made a career out of investing in companies in just one industry. Of course, they minimize their risk of concentrating in just one area by understanding that area very, very well. If you have special areas of knowledge and/or interest, this is a wonderful approach to pursue. Unfortunately, this is the advice I give to my MBA students. I am assuming when I recommend this strategy that they have at least some rudimentary ability and understanding on how to value a company.

But my students can't all be above-average analysts. So there's another strategy they seem to like even more than the "be a little lazy" investment plan. What if they're just not that good at making estimates of earnings or guessing about future growth rates? Sure, it will be helpful and a nice advantage to spend most of their time analyzing smaller companies where there is less competition from the big institutions to find bargain priced stocks. It should also help them not to try to analyze hundreds of companies but to concentrate their efforts on just a few companies where they feel most confident about their knowledge of the business and where they have a good understanding of the industry. But what if that's not enough? What if they're just not that talented and their analytical abilities are only average? What do I tell those students? Well, I tell them the same thing that any good professor would. I tell them to spend the weekend with my in-laws.

In my first book, I recounted the story about the strange and profitable weekend habits of my wife's parents (aka "the in-laws"). Yes, they *could* spend their weekends watching ball games and puttering around the house. But instead they wander around country auctions, antiques stores, and estate sales looking for antiques or art they can buy at bargain prices. When they look for these bargains, they're not really looking for paintings by the next Picasso. That would require them to predict which undiscovered artists' works will be worth a lot more someday. They also aren't trying to figure out whether eighteenth-century French furniture is about to skyrocket in value. That would require them to predict the future, too. Instead, they try to make their challenge much easier.

Whether they find a beautiful antique desk or a pretty impressionist painting, they really ask only one question before buying: are there comparable pieces of furniture or paintings that have recently sold at auction (or to dealers) at prices far above the potential purchase price? That's it.[1] That doesn't mean that their knowledge of art and antiques doesn't help them to make money. But many people can acquire that same knowledge. Their real edge comes from taking this knowledge and applying it in places off the beaten path. While these places are a bit tougher to find, less

---

1. Apparently, no one needed to teach *them* about "relative value."

competition from other informed collectors creates the opportunity to find undiscovered bargains.

As it happens, the stock market has its own version of country auctions and estate sales. This area of the investment world is often referred to as *special situation investing*. These are places, I tell my students, where it's not so important to be able to predict the future. The main challenge is merely to find some of these out-of-the-way corners of the market in the first place. Knowing where to look, rather than extraordinary talent, is the most important part of finding bargains in some of these less well-followed areas.

One little Wall Street backwater is the area known as *spinoffs*. Companies that need to raise money to expand their business generally have two choices. They can either borrow money or sell a piece of the business. If a company is big enough and needs millions to expand, it can choose to sell shares in the business to a wide range of investors through something called a *public offering*. In most cases, the company will hire an investment banker to help organize a sale of these shares through a network of Wall Street investment firms. The company provides background information about itself to these investment firms, who actively sell the shares to their clients and get paid based upon a percentage of the money raised.

Spinoffs work a bit differently. Larger companies that already have publicly traded shares often are in many different lines of business. Sometimes a company may want to separate these various businesses from one another. This could happen because one of the businesses is doing poorly and management views a separation from the "good" business as a wise move. In other instances, the business is just a small piece of the entire company and management doesn't want to waste time and effort on the smaller division. Sometimes management may feel that the stock market is "confused" by the combination of two disparate businesses and that the company's stock price does not fully reflect the value of each of the businesses. But whatever the reason, rather than sell one of the divisions, the company may decide to just distribute the shares in that division to its existing shareholders through a *spinoff transaction*.

Unlike a *public offering*, though, where investment firms actively sell shares to clients, in the case of a spinoff, the shares are distributed directly to shareholders. These holders never asked for shares in the new spinoff and are much more likely to sell in the months after they receive them than people who ask for shares in the usual public offering supported by a Wall Street investment firm. In addition, Wall Street firms don't make money from the distribution of spinoff shares and therefore don't usually provide research coverage for new spinoffs. This lack of research creates an even greater potential for mispricing of the new shares. Then again, if you're looking to buy some bargain shares, this could be a very good thing!

Another great source for bargains includes the unlikely niche of stocks coming out of *bankruptcy*. This is where a company doesn't have enough cash to pay off its debts. Instead, in a bankruptcy proceeding, the company's creditors may receive shares of stock in the business, instead of cash, to satisfy the debt obligation. You might imagine what a supplier of napkins to a bankrupt restaurant chain (which originally expected to get paid in cash) would do if, instead, it got paid with shares of stock in the restaurant company. (Hint: It *could* try to analyze what they were worth, but much more likely it would just sell them!). The effect on the share price is similar to what often takes place with spinoffs where unwanted and unanalyzed stocks create a greater chance for mispriced bargains.

Other special situation areas with the potential to create even more bargain opportunities include *restructurings, mergers, liquidations, asset sales, distributions, rights offerings, recapitalizations, options, smaller foreign securities, complex securities*, and many more. In fact, I wrote a whole (poorly titled) book about these types of investments,[2] and I spend a good amount of time teaching my MBA class about them each year. These special situations involving companies going through various types of extraordinary change clearly provide fertile ground for bargain hunters.

Unfortunately, this area still presents some serious roadblocks for many investors. First, since the individual special situations are fairly unique, each investment requires a reasonable amount of time and effort to find and evaluate. Second, although I tell my students to concentrate on situations where the bargain is pretty obvious (thus cutting down on the necessity to be a good forecaster), some basic valuation skills are clearly still necessary. Finally, another major impediment, relevant to both large and small investors, is that many of these off-the-beaten-path situations are relatively small in size. They may be too small for institutional investors to bother with, and since most Wall Street firms don't provide research in this area, smaller investors are totally on their own when trying to analyze them.

---

2. *You Can Be a Stock Market Genius* (Simon & Schuster, 1997).

But don't worry. You really only have to understand what comes next, because here's the main point of the entire chapter. When it comes to the stock market, investors who are willing to do a little work have plenty of ways to gain an advantage by simply changing the game. They can manage smaller amounts of money (millions as opposed to billions), research some of the thousands of smaller companies where there is less competition, concentrate their portfolio in just a few investments where they have the most knowledge and confidence, and invest in special situations where the advantages come mostly from just looking in the right places.

But what do most professional investment managers do? None of these things! As we'll examine next chapter, they're all stuck out on the golf course competing with Tiger Woods!

SUMMARY

1. In the stock market, there are plenty of ways for investors willing to do some work to gain an edge.

2. Most professional investment managers don't (or can't) take advantage of any of them!

3. Next chapter, we'll see what most professional managers actually do instead.

4. Later, we'll figure out what you should do (especially if you don't want to do any work)!

CHAPTER

SIX

So Dorothy, the Scarecrow, and the rest of the gang are on a wooded path on their way to the Wicked Witch's castle when they come upon a sign that reads ominously, "I'd Turn Back if I Were You!" Of course, the Cowardly Lion immediately turns and starts to run. As a kid just watching on television, I was already scared out of my mind, so I wanted to start running, too! Though I was still young, it was easy to figure out that things were about to get worse. Well, in case you didn't realize it, we're on a path of our own and our sign is coming up right about . . . now.

But before we decide whether to pass by or not, let's take a quick look back and review where we've been. We started our journey with the secret to successful investing: figure out the *value* of something and then— pay a lot less. Unfortunately, as it turns out, it's really hard to figure out the value of a business. It's difficult enough to figure out what a company is going to earn next quarter or next year, but we have to make guesses about earnings for the next ten, twenty, or thirty years. Even after we come up with these guesses, very small changes in our estimates for future earnings, growth rates, and discount rates (reflecting our level of confidence in our earnings estimates) make a huge difference in our ultimate estimates of value.

Other methods, such as relative value, acquisition value, liquidation value, and sum-of-the-parts analysis, are difficult to use and can often lead to seriously inaccurate estimates of value. Even when we simplify things and compare our investment alternatives to the risk-free rate and to each other, we still must rely on the accuracy of our estimates and our ability to assess our level of confidence in those estimates. Needless to say, making earnings estimates, risk assessments, and comparisons for not just one but dozens or even hundreds of companies, and doing it well, must be really hard.

In fact, Ben Graham in his *Intelligent Investor* warned individual investors against trying to analyze individual stocks on their own by thinking they can succeed merely by bringing "a little extra knowledge and cleverness" to the investment process. He suggested that instead of realizing "a little better than normal results, you may well find that you have done worse."

Luckily for my MBA students, on the other hand,

with time, effort, and study, there are a number of things *they* can do to change the game and overcome some of these difficult investment challenges. Not so luckily, most professional investment managers don't (or can't) take advantage of any of them. Instead, as we're about to examine, they do something else. But if, as Jack Nicholson might say, "you can't handle the truth!" then this would be the time "I'd turn back if I were you!"

Fine, I'm glad you're still reading. So here's the deal. Most individual investors who decide not to do it themselves and who want professional management for their stock market investments place their money in *mutual funds*. For those who don't already know, these are investment vehicles that pool the money from many investors into one fund that is managed by a professional manager (or by a management team). Investors can generally choose from funds that are *actively managed* or *passively managed*. In general, active managers try to beat the market by buying a portfolio of stocks that will outperform the stock market averages. Passive management, often referred to as an *index approach*, is simply a strategy designed to replicate the returns of a particular stock market index (such as the S&P 500 or Russell 1000) by buying all or most of the stocks in that index. This is usually done for a very low management fee (or nonmanagement fee, I guess).

For our purposes in this chapter (and because we can probably figure out how to get average returns), let's just talk about actively managed mutual funds and the managers who try to beat the market. Before we start, though, and despite what I'm about to say, let me make clear that most mutual fund managers are hard-working professionals and extremely nice people (just go with me on this). The problem is that their job is really tough. Let's see why.

Here are the basics. Most actively managed mutual funds charge fees and expenses based on the size of the fund, usually 1 percent to 2 percent of the total assets under management. This means that the more assets a fund has, the more money the management company makes. As you might suspect, this incentive to gather more assets isn't necessarily good for investors.

In the last chapter we learned that there is an advantage to looking at smaller companies. These companies are often too small for large investment funds to buy and for Wall Street firms to spend money on doing research. Less competition from other buyers and less available Wall Street research often mean a greater opportunity to find bargain-priced stocks among these lesser followed small capitalization companies. Since, as we've already learned, there are thousands of companies with market capitalizations below $1 billion both in the United States and internationally, smaller investors have a big advantage. Being able to choose from thousands of additional choices with less competition from large investors is a luxury that successful investors like Warren Buffett wish they still had. Yet the goal of most mutual funds is to gather as many assets as possible. Chances are that by the time you've heard of a successful mutual fund, it already has many hundreds of millions or billions under management and can no longer take advantage of some of these smaller investment opportunities.

The next problem is that most of these actively managed funds own between fifty and two hundred stocks in their portfolio. We just spent a lot of time discussing how difficult it must be to do a good job analyzing the value of a business. Understanding a company and its industry well enough to project earnings, growth rates, and discount rates far into the future for even one company is a tough challenge. To have this kind of extraordinary insight into a handful of companies at any one time is probably more than any fund manager or management team can really ask for. But that's only part of the problem. Many of the companies that *can* be effectively valued might not be available at an attractive price. To provide some measure of good performance for the fund, at least a few of the companies that *can* be effectively valued must also be priced by the market at bargain levels. Since it's so difficult to find even a few companies that can be both accurately valued *and* available at a good price, one thing seems pretty clear: once a fund gets to its twentieth or fiftieth favorite pick, it's not likely that very much extra value is being added to the portfolio.

But there are a number of reasons why most funds still own so many stocks. First, they view having a diversified portfolio of many stocks as an advantage. It's difficult for individual investors to purchase and keep track of a portfolio of fifty to two hundred stocks. A mutual fund with a professionally managed, widely diversified portfolio provides a service that most individuals have difficulty replicating on their own. This diversification helps make sure that a handful of bad stock choices don't have an outsized negative influence on overall investment returns. (Then again, this kind of diversification also helps ensure that a handful of *good* stock picks don't have an outsized *positive* influence on overall investment returns, either!)

Second, there are various regulatory rules and practical limitations that encourage mutual funds to own dozens or hundreds of stocks. Some rules require certain stock positions to be less than 5 percent of the entire fund, and others limit the percentage of a company that can be owned by one fund to no more than 10 percent of the total shares outstanding. Oftentimes, buying even 5 percent of a company's outstanding shares can present difficulties. Accumulating a large position in one company can push the stock price significantly higher when the fund is trying to buy shares and push the price lower when it tries to sell. This usually makes it more practical for most funds with hundreds of millions or billions in assets to just buy a large number of smaller-sized positions in companies with larger market capitalizations.

For funds that specialize in smaller-capitalization companies, and there are some, buying a portfolio with many stocks is almost a necessity. While these funds are designed to take advantage of the greater opportunities and choices among the thousands of smaller companies, they are also generally forced to buy many dozens or hundreds of small company stocks. Due to each company's smaller size, it's really not possible to invest a large amount of money in any particular stock. As a result, much of the advantage of being able to find a few great opportunities among smaller companies is lost by diluting a few excellent stock ideas with fifty or a hundred other stock holdings that are not as attractive.

But the main reason most mutual funds choose to

own dozens or hundreds of stocks is very simple: they don't like to lose. Most mutual funds are judged by whether they can beat the returns of a particular market index. In the last chapter, we discussed one way to do this: concentrate on a few of your favorite ideas. As we just discussed, funds specializing in smaller-capitalization stocks can't really do this due to the small size of each individual company. But funds that invest mostly in large-capitalization stocks can. Through hard work, industry expertise, and special insights (even though it's harder than with small-cap stocks), it's still possible for talented managers to find a handful of bargains among large-capitalization stocks and invest billions of dollars. But the few managers who do this are taking a big risk.

The returns from a portfolio of only ten or twenty stocks can vary widely from the returns of a market index that contains a portfolio of five hundred or a thousand stocks. As you might expect (and as we'll discuss in more detail later), a portfolio of hundreds of large-capitalization stocks will usually do pretty average. A portfolio of ten or twenty favorite picks has the chance to do well above average. But, unfortunately, it also has the chance to do well *below* average. Even a very talented manager who makes excellent stock picks over the long term can trail the market averages for years at a time. In fact, this is almost a certainty with a concentrated portfolio.

But the reality is that a manager who significantly underperforms the market averages for two or three years has a good chance of losing most of his or her investors! Most investors just can't figure out which managers fall behind the market averages because of bad luck or bad timing and which managers fall behind due to a poor investment process and a lack of talent. Most don't wait around to figure out which is which. Like the Cowardly Lion, they just turn and run! And no investors means no business! Over the long term, managing a concentrated portfolio may be a great way to beat the market averages, but over shorter time horizons it's also a great way to risk your business and your career. As a result, only a few brave souls choose this route in the mutual fund world. It's just much safer for most managers to buy a widely diversified portfolio of many stocks that are more likely to closely mirror the major market averages and much less likely to fall significantly behind.

As you might suspect, special situation investing follows pretty much the same story line. By definition, each of these special situations, in which a company is going through some sort of extraordinary change, is unique. Many of the opportunities involve smaller companies or situations where there is a limited opportunity to invest large sums of capital. Since these situations have to be evaluated and researched extensively on a one-off basis, often require a specialized skill set to analyze, and are usually too small for larger funds to benefit from, very few mutual fund managers can spend the time and effort necessary to take advantage of this area of investment opportunity.

In other words, most mutual fund managers are effectively shut out from their best chances to beat the market. Most can't take advantage of the thousands of opportunities available in lesser analyzed, smaller-capitalization stocks. For practical and business reasons, most can't concentrate their portfolio on just their few best ideas. As for special situations, as we just discussed, these are largely out of the picture, too! In short, most fund managers are stuck buying a portfolio of between fifty and two hundred of the largest, most widely followed stocks.

The result is predictable: most don't beat the market. In fact, because of management fees, most don't even match the market averages. On average and over time, actively managed funds lose to passive index funds by approximately the amount of their higher management fees.

But for investors it gets even worse. Most investors

have no idea why or how an active manager chooses the stocks in his portfolio. As we've seen, many estimates and assumptions go into each and every investment choice. What investors do know is how a particular fund has performed over the last few years. Has it beaten the market? Has it beaten other similar funds? Since the end result is pretty much all investors get to see, that's what they use to make their investment decisions.

Unfortunately, it turns out that relying on recent good or bad performance to make investment decisions isn't such a smart way to go. Even professional allocators of capital seem to chase recent good performance and run from underperforming managers. Several research studies tracked the investments of these large, "professionally" managed fund allocators (such as foundations, endowments, and pension plans) and analyzed their decisions to hire and fire investment managers. The results weren't pretty.[1]

Most managers were hired due to good recent performance. Most managers that were fired had recently

---

1. Amit Goyal and Sunil Wahal, "The Selection and Termination of Investment Management Firms by Plan Sponsors," *Journal of Finance*, Vol. 63, No. 4, August 2008 (this study followed more than 3,400 professionals); see also Stewart, Neuman, Knittel, and Heisler, "Absence of Value: An Analysis of Investment Allocation by Institutional Plan Sponsors," *Financial Analysts Journal*, November/December 2009.

underperformed the market averages.[2] In short, these "professional" fund allocators would have been better off staying home! In the years following hire and fire decisions, the recently fired managers significantly outperformed the market while the recently hired didn't show any outperformance at all.

And that's how the "professionals" did at picking managers! Individual investors make even worse decisions. The best-performing stock mutual fund of the last decade earned more than 18 percent annually (by the way, this fund runs a concentrated portfolio of fewer than twenty-five large-cap stocks). This is particularly impressive since the market as measured by the S&P 500 was actually down close to 1 percent per year between 2000 and 2009. Yet the average investor in this same fund managed to *lose* 11 percent per year over those ten years.[3] How? Pretty much after every period in which the fund did well, investors piled in. After every period in which the fund did poorly, investors ran for the exits. So the average investor managed to lose money in the best-performing fund purely by buying and selling the fund at just the wrong

2. For the two years before hiring, managers had outperformed by 7 percent; before firing, they had underperformed by 2.1 percent.

3. Morningstar study quoted in the *Wall Street Journal*, December 31, 2009, "Best Stock Fund of the Decade."

times![4] While this is an extreme example, individual investors follow the same pattern as professionals. They pull money out *after* the market or a manager does poorly. They put money in only *after* the market is already up or a manager has outperformed.

On average, because of poor timing decisions (with regard to both market moves and manager selection) and the drag of management fees, investors can't even match the market averages. You might intuitively think that when you combine everyone's returns, the end result would have to be average. But over the last two decades ending in 2009, the S&P 500 averaged returns of 8.2 percent, yet mutual fund investors earned much less—approximately two-thirds of that amount, according to one study, and less than half that amount, according to another.[5] The rest went to management fees and bad market timing decisions. Over two decades those lost returns (even using the two-thirds estimate) actually translate into half as much in profits![6]

---

4. While the returns for this fund were spectacular, it didn't help that they were also more volatile than the average fund (though this should have been expected from such a concentrated fund!).

5. See "Quantitative Analysis of Investor Behavior," Dalbar, 2010, and Friesen and Sapp, "Mutual Fund Flows and Investor Returns: An Empirical Examination of Fund Investor Timing Ability," *Journal of Banking and Finance*, Vol. 31, 2007.

6. On a starting $1 investment you would earn only $1.89 in profits versus $3.83.

So bad market timing aside (we'll try to deal with that a bit later), it's pretty clear that professionals and amateurs have a hard time figuring out which active managers to invest with. Even Morningstar, the most influential company in the mutual fund rating business, has generously admitted that ranking funds based solely on low expenses would have done a more consistent job of predicting future good performance than their proprietary star rating system.[7] Yet even with all this bad news, each decade approximately 30 percent of active funds do manage to outperform the S&P 500. Isn't there some way to find those guys ahead of time?

Well, it might be possible, but there are some major roadblocks that need to be overcome. Looking at just the top quartile (best-performing 25 percent) of managers over a recent decade,[8] almost all of these top-performing managers (96 percent) spent at least one three-year period during that decade in the bottom half of the performance rankings. Even more telling, 79 percent spent at least three years in the bottom quartile (bottom 25 percent of managers) and

---

7. "How Expense Ratios and Star Ratings Predict Success," *Morningstar Fund Spy*, August 9, 2010.

8. Source: Davis Advisors (1/1/00–12/31/09).

a staggering 47 percent spent at least three years in the bottom 10 percent. In other words, even the best-performing managers go through long periods of significant underperformance.

Unfortunately, this makes perfect sense, since to beat the market (as represented by the S&P 500 in this case), you must invest differently than the market. At a minimum, you can't invest in exactly the same stocks in exactly the same proportion as a market index and still beat it! Even if a manager has talent and his strategy is sensible, stocks fluctuate at different times and in different ways, so long-term outperformance due to a strategy that differs from the index is almost always accompanied by lengthy periods of underperformance. Since almost all investors chase recent good performance and run from recent poor performance, it's no wonder they have a hard time sticking with even those managers who eventually end up with the best long-term records.

Although it's probably already too late, there's one final problem before we beat this horse to death. (Hey, I warned you, and you walked right by the sign anyway!) As we've just discussed, mutual fund managers who have been successful in the recent past attract lots of investors. (After all, it's hard to throw money at managers who have been unsuccessful or only average!)

The problem is that it's generally more difficult to manage larger sums of capital. When a fund is smaller, it can take advantage of some smaller opportunities. A larger universe of stocks to select from gives a manager more chances to find bargains. Smaller situations can still have a major impact on a small fund's portfolio. In addition, a manager generally can concentrate more in his favorite situations when he can choose to own both larger and smaller stocks. Having the ability to invest in smaller situations also generally means a manager is not forced to spread his investments over a larger number of stocks and so may not have to move as far down a list of favorites.

But once hundreds of millions or billions come in the door, things have to change. Many times the smaller situations and opportunities that helped make a manager successful and attracted all that money in the first place are now too small to have a major impact or, because of their small size, are off the table completely. As Warren Buffett has said, "It's a huge structural advantage not to have a lot of money. I think I could make 50% a year on a million, no, I know I could. I guarantee that."[9] Of course, all of us would rather have billions and make less than 50 percent, but you get the basic idea.

---

9. Warren Buffett, quoted in *BusinessWeek*, June 25, 1999.

Investing with the managers who have performed the best and attracted all the money is probably a great way to win the last war, just not a great strategy for beating the market going forward.

So what is?

SUMMARY

1. You shouldn't have passed by that sign.

2. Given how the system operates, it's very hard for active mutual fund managers to beat the market.

3. Given how both professional and individual investors operate, it's very hard for them to stick with even the best managers. Winning strategies, by definition, must deviate from the market indexes. As a result, almost all good managers go through extended periods of underperformance. Almost all investors run away from managers who underperform.

4. By the time we figure out who the best managers are, their funds have usually accumulated a large amount of assets under management, making it

much more difficult for them to continue with the strategy that made them successful in the first place. (This may be one reason why the top performing funds from one decade bear no resemblance to the top performing funds of the next!)

5. It's hard to value stocks. It's hard to pick winning mutual funds. Is that really the *big secret for the small investor*? (Don't worry, if it were, my publisher would have already killed me.)

FOR ADVANCED STUDENTS ONLY
(PEOPLE WITH UNUSUAL AMOUNTS OF
PATIENCE ARE ALSO WELCOME)

One thing that has always bothered me about attempts to rank manager performance is the issue of benchmarking. Benchmarking is the practice of comparing a manager's performance over various time periods to a particular market index or to other managers with similar invest-ment styles. As we've discussed, a manager's challenge is to value a company (or a particular security, in the case of non-equity managers) and then to buy it if it is available at a large discount to that value. It is impossible for even the best managers or management teams to do a good job valuing all companies. The best an active manager can hope to do is to stick within his areas of expertise and to do a good job valuing (to be very generous) a few dozen companies (or investment opportunities) at any one time.

As we've also discussed, one hurdle a stock selection must meet before it can be considered a good investment is to beat the risk-free rate available from the U.S. government (we have defined this as at least 6 percent per year over time when the ten-year bond is yielding less than 6 percent and higher when the government yield is above 6 percent). The investment must beat this risk-free alternative by enough to compensate for the fact that future earnings of a company are not guaranteed. In other words, to qualify as a good investment, the return from that investment must compensate for the added risk taken plus some additional amount.

Being able to identify investment opportunities that provide a return sufficiently higher than the risk-free rate to more than compensate for the risk taken is a very valuable skill. Essentially this skill comes down to being very good at valuing businesses and/or securities and then having the discipline to buy only when the particular investment is available at a large enough discount to the calculated value. Since over longer periods of time (but

87

usually within several years) the market generally gets valuations right, good valuation work is eventually rewarded with the chance to sell at a fair price.

But here's what bothers me. A manager who is talented at locating good investments (as defined above) may still not beat the market or his competition. At times, other companies in the marketplace may be available at even bigger discounts to the ones our manager chooses to buy (since our manager can only choose from those companies that he has the ability and time to value). The stock prices of the companies in his portfolio might turn out to be more or less volatile than the market or the stocks in the portfolios of his competition. Nevertheless, our manager could be a superstar. On a risk-adjusted basis (taking into account the quality of our manager's valuation skills), he could be one of the world's best investors. His benchmark should not be beating the market or other managers. The evaluation of the risk taken should not be the volatility of his portfolio. His benchmark should be his ability to, over a long period of time, contribute returns meaningfully above the risk-free rate after adjusting for the extra risks taken (this evaluation of risk assumes we had the ability to assess his analytical process correctly). This does not guarantee, however, that his returns will be better than the market's. It only means that he has the talent to consistently add value above and beyond the risks taken.[10]

As you might imagine, managers who must compete on a shorter-term basis with the benchmark returns of stock market indexes and other managers can get distracted from looking at investing in the pure fashion of just finding good investments. They may well have to make some of the compromises already discussed (like buying many stocks or mirroring what everyone else is doing) to avoid falling too far behind and risking their business. After twenty or thirty years of solid performance, despite these business roadblocks and an evaluation system that uses the wrong benchmarks for measuring performance, we might identify our superstar manager anyway (assuming he's still in business). Then again, by this point, this discovery may no longer be all that timely or helpful. What a shame.

---

10. In other words, a talented manager could earn 10 percent per year at very low risk and easily beat the risk-free rate even after adjusting for the extra risks taken. That could be a great performance even if the market was up 12 percent per year during this same period. Why? The 10 percent return, if it was earned as a result of the discipline and valuation skills of our manager, could have been much more certain than the market's 12 percent return.

Alas, back to the real world. While we may now have a little better idea what to look for, it's still not likely that we can find these superstar managers ahead of time. They do have certain characteristics in common, but unfortunately, it's still a know-'em-when-I-see-'em type of thing. But don't worry, we *can* still learn to beat the market and almost all active mutual fund managers. While not perfect, that's got to be worth something! So, let's see how . . .

spent seven years in summer camp (not all at once). While to many that might not sound so great, it was. Sure, we didn't have the best facilities, the food was awful, and yes, the bugs and the bug juice were in their natural habitat. But we got to play sports all day long. If you didn't win in the morning, there was always another game in the afternoon. If today didn't work out, tomorrow was a taps and reveille away. It was heaven.

The baseball field was a little tricky, though. Half of left field was on a steep hill. The left fielder had to stand unevenly with his left foot flat on the ground and his right foot planted up the hill. Right field wasn't any better. There was a large tree hanging over it, and to play it well you had to figure out which way the ball would deflect off the branches. As for center field, where exactly that collection of large rocks poked out of the ground was especially important to know (but even more important if you played soccer, since center also doubled as the soccer field).

Okay, maybe it wasn't quite heaven.[1] But we learned to deal with the obstacles and the imperfections (if not the bugs), and in the end we made it work. So that's what we're going to try to do now. We'll have to overcome some obstacles, our own imperfections, and a playing field that's not exactly even, but in the end we can make it work. We might even add one to the win column—that is, if you think beating the market and almost all professional managers counts as a victory.

But how are we going to do that? As we've already learned, if we can't figure out the value of something, then we can't buy it at an intelligent price. For most investors, figuring out the value of a business is simply out of the question—to do a good job is just much too tough. What about getting an expert to do it for us? Sorry, we've already covered that. Due to fees and the way the investment business works, most active mutual fund managers underperform the market. As for the few who do end up beating the market, we can't find them ahead of time. Finding them right *after* they've

---

1. One of my favorite *Twilight Zone* episodes is the one where a biker (think Harley) and an elderly couple are watching an endless slide show of the couple's vacation in Mexico. The upshot: one man's heaven is another man's hell. Though they were both in the same place, the couple had made it to heaven and the biker had been sentenced to hell.

outperformed doesn't help because most don't continue with the outperformance. So what's the answer?

Well, one common solution that works well for many individual investors is to buy what are known as index funds. These are funds designed to match the returns of popular indexes, less a very small fee. The Standard & Poor's 500 Index (S&P 500) consists of approximately five hundred of the largest publicly traded companies in the United States as selected by Standard & Poor's to represent a broad variety of businesses and industries. Another popular index, known as the Russell 1000, is basically the one thousand largest publicly traded companies based in the United States. There are all kinds of other indexes covering smaller companies, international companies, companies in specific industries, and many others.

But by far the most popular indexes are the ones that cover the largest companies. When people talk about beating the market, they usually are referring to beating an index like the S&P 500 or the Russell 1000. And when people choose to invest in U.S. index funds, likewise, most of the money flows into funds based on these two indexes or their equivalents. So what are these indexes, really?

The big picture is that the S&P 500 Index and the Russell 1000 Index are constructed based upon the market capitalization of the individual companies in each index. In other words, they are considered *market-cap-weighted* indexes, and it's important to carefully examine what this means. While the Russell 1000 Index is roughly the one thousand largest publicly traded companies in the United States, those one thousand companies do not carry equal weight in the index. Companies with larger market capitalizations are weighted more heavily. So the index is influenced much more by companies with market capitalizations toward the top of the list than by those toward the bottom.

This is an incredibly important fact to understand. For instance, with regard to the S&P 500 Index, while the largest twenty companies out of the five hundred represent only 4 percent of the companies on the list, these twenty companies represent approximately one-third of the market value of the entire index. The largest company of the S&P 500 represents approximately 3.5 percent of the index, while the smallest accounts for only 8/1000 of 1 percent (.008%). In other words, for these indexes, size matters.

But that's okay; in many ways this makes sense. If we want to know how all owners of U.S. stocks did in aggregate, a market-cap-weighted index such as the Russell 1000 is actually a pretty good indicator. Those one thousand stocks represent approximately 90 percent of the market value of all publicly traded U.S.-based stocks. If the index goes up 5 percent, that means that the aggregate market value of publicly traded U.S.-based companies held by investors also went up approximately 5 percent. So, all in all, it's not a bad choice for an index when you want to know how the market is doing.

But, more important, it's also a great choice if you want to beat most active mutual fund managers. As we've already discussed, largely because of an average of 1 to 2 percent in annual fees and expenses, only about 30 percent of active managers beat the Russell 1000 or S&P 500 indexes over time.[2] Since there really isn't a reliable way to figure out who the winning managers will be ahead of time, the odds say to invest in the index. There are now many low-cost ways to invest in one of these indexes through both mutual funds and a special type of closed-end mutual fund known as an *ETF*.[3] One of the many great attributes of market cap weighting is that it can be very efficiently and cost-effectively implemented. As stocks in the index go up in price, their weightings are automatically adjusted by the increase in the stock price—no trading is necessary. When stocks in the index go down in price, they

---

2. The long-term returns of the two indexes are roughly equivalent.

3. We'll discuss *ETFs* (exchange-traded funds) a bit later.

immediately have a lower market capitalization, and this also is reflected in the index without a single trade. As a result, the fees for some of these index-based mutual funds can actually run below 0.1 percent per year.

But before we say, "Case closed, let's just buy the index fund," we should pay another visit to Warren Buffett's mentor and the acknowledged father of security analysis, Benjamin Graham. We first met him in Chapter 2 when we discussed the concept of margin of safety (i.e., leaving a big space between the value of what you are buying and the price you pay). But Graham also provided us with a now famous metaphor for the best way to think about stock price movements. He suggested that when looking at the fluctuations of stock prices, we should imagine that we are partners in a business with an emotional (and sometimes crazy) guy named *Mr. Market*.

Mr. Market is subject to wild mood swings. Each day he offers to buy our share of the business or sell us his share of the business at a particular price. There are days when Mr. Market is in such a good mood that he names a price that is much higher than the true worth of the business. On those days, Graham says it would probably make sense to sell Mr. Market our share of the business. On other days, he is in such a poor mood that he names a very low price for the business. On those days, we might want to take advantage of our crazy partner and buy Mr. Market's share of the business.

What Graham meant was that markets are emotional. They often go to extremes of pessimism and optimism, and prices can and often do fluctuate wildly and significantly over short periods of time. (If you have doubts, a look at the range of prices for the individual stock of your choice over any fifty-two-week period should quickly confirm this!) But Graham pointed out that the long-term value of a business can't possibly change as often and as drastically as changes in stock prices seem to indicate. These emotional price swings, which sometimes produce stock prices at a big discount (or large premium) to the value of the underlying business, can be exploited by an investor who focuses only on value. In fact, Buffett considers Graham's contributions with regard to the idea of investing with a large margin of safety and the metaphor of viewing stock price fluctuations in the context of Mr. Market as the two most important concepts in investing.

So what does this have to do with index funds? Well, a lot, actually. Here's why. If Graham and Buffett are right, over the short term at least, stock prices can sometimes reflect emotions rather than value. In other words, there are times when people get excited by the prospects for a particular company or industry group and overpay for these stocks. At the same time, there are often other companies or industries where investors get unduly pessimistic. These stocks can get oversold and trade at prices much lower than fair value. How does a market-cap-weighted index such as the S&P 500 or Russell 1000 deal with these situations?

Not well. Remember, a market-cap-weighted index ends up having a larger weighting in stocks that increase in value and a smaller weighting in companies whose prices decrease. As Mr. Market gets overly excited about certain companies and overpays, their weighting in a market-cap-weighted index rises. Consequently, an index fund that owns these same stocks ends up being more heavily weighted in these overpriced stocks. If Mr. Market is overly pessimistic about particular companies or industries, the opposite happens. The stock prices of these companies fall below fair value, and the index and the accompanying index fund effectively own less of these bargain-priced stocks.

In fact, the effect of owning too much of the overpriced stocks and too little of the bargain-priced stocks is actually built into the market-cap-weighting system. Again, as stocks move up in price, we own more of them through the index. As stocks move down in price, we own less of them. So as Internet stocks moved up in price and market capitalization in the late 1990s, the major indexes became more heavily weighted in this overpriced sector. The more expensive and overpriced they got, the more the index owned. This is the exact opposite of what an investor should want. On the other hand, many companies in traditional industries with solid earnings and good prospects were ignored by the market. Many of these companies were priced well below fair value. Unfortunately, the market-cap-weighted index effectively owned too little of these bargain companies—their low market capitalizations resulted in index weightings that were much too low.

In effect, if emotions really do drive certain stocks to be overpriced and others to be underpriced, a market cap weighting guarantees that we will own an inferior portfolio. We don't even have to identify which stocks are overpriced and which are underpriced. As long as we know that at least some stocks are mispriced relative to their fair value, weighting by market cap will ensure that we buy too much of the overpriced ones and too little of the bargains.

On the other hand, if stocks are efficiently priced based on all currently available information (as my professors from the 1970s taught me), then market cap weighting should work perfectly. We'll own just the right amount of each stock, prices and market capitalizations will accurately reflect the true value of each company (given the information available to investors) and as a result, on average, stocks will be weighted correctly in the index.[4]

Well, let's just say that I side with Graham, Buffett, and common sense on this one. We've spent a lot of time discussing how very small changes in assumptions about future earnings, growth rates, and discount rates for a particular business can make for extreme changes in our estimates for the value of that business. So it shouldn't come as a surprise when a little more optimism drives a stock's price higher or when a touch of pessimism helps us justify lower prices. If we're willing to assume that stocks do sometimes get mispriced due to emotion, then there should be some logical ways to create an index that doesn't suffer from the same built-in flaws of market cap weighting. More

---

4. Of course, my professors didn't really think that all stocks were fairly valued, because to a large degree the future is uncertain. They just believed that all currently available information was already reflected in stock prices. Therefore, new developments could still drive future prices higher or lower; it's just that those new developments were unpredictable and therefore future price movements would be random. So some stocks would eventually go higher and some lower, but in a random fashion. In an index, they figured, those random movements would cancel each other out and on average the index would be fairly priced. (Oh, forget it! It's all gibberish anyway! You're better off just knowing that Mr. Market screws up sometimes and a market-cap-weighted index systematically buys too much of the expensive stuff and too little of the cheap stuff!)

important, an index that doesn't systematically own too much of the overpriced stocks and too little of the bargain-priced ones should provide us with even better long-term investment returns than the market-cap-weighted indexes. Since market cap weighting, flawed as it is, appears to handily beat most active managers over time, that's actually pretty exciting.

There's even one simple solution that seems pretty obvious. What if we just weighted all stocks in the index equally? In that way, we could eliminate the bias that mispricing individual stocks based on emotion would cause. So for the S&P 500, we could still own all five hundred stocks in the index, but in equal weights. Each company would represent 0.2 percent (1/500th) of the index regardless of its market capitalization. Sure, we'd still own too much of some companies that were overpriced and too little of some bargain-priced stocks, but we'd also own more of some bargains than a market-cap-weighted index would tell us to own and less of some overpriced stocks. Over time, rather than systematically buying too much of the overpriced stocks and too little of the underpriced ones, like in a cap-weighted index, in an *equally weighted index*, our pricing errors would be random and should cancel one another out over time. In fact, there's already some evidence that equal weighting does actually improve returns.

Over the last two decades, at least theoretically, an S&P 500 equally weighted index would have indeed outperformed the capitalization-weighted index by an average of 1.5 percent to 2 percent per year before factoring in expenses.[5] But, unfortunately, you'll have to keep reading, because it's not quite that simple. There are still a few problems with the equal-weighting process. First, since stock prices move every day, those equal weights are constantly getting thrown out of whack. If you hold 0.2 percent of your portfolio in each stock on day one, if some stocks move up and some down, or individual stocks move up or down in unequal amounts, what started out as equal weighting will no longer be equal.

An equally weighted portfolio, to stay that way, must be constantly rebalanced. As prices change and readjustments need to be made, this can lead to a high turnover of stocks, higher trading costs, and more taxes. Also, some of the smaller stocks in the index are not that liquid (i.e., not that many shares of some of the smaller companies in the S&P 500 or the Russell 1000 may trade each day, making them difficult to buy or sell without moving the price). As a result, while there

---

5. Some studies show this is also true for the last eighty years. See Edward F. McQuarrie, "Fundamentally Indexed or Fundamentally Misconceived," *Journal of Investing*, Winter 2008.

is estimated to be over $1 trillion invested in market-cap-weighted indexes, if even a small portion of this amount was switched to equally weighted indexes, it would render this strategy impractical. On the other hand, most people haven't switched yet, so feel free to go ahead and invest![6]

But before you do, consider some other choices. Equally weighting stocks isn't the only way to overcome some of the built-in flaws of market-cap-weighted indexes. There are also a number of what are known as *fundamentally weighted index strategies* that have some definite advantages over simply equally weighting all stocks. For these strategies, instead of using market capitalization to decide how much to buy of each stock in the index, other measures of economic size are used. The size of a company can be measured by the amount of sales the company has, by earnings, by a company's book value (essentially its assets minus its liabilities), by dividends, or by any number or combination of other measures of economic size. The idea behind these indexes is to avoid the problems that come from using market capitalization (price multiplied by shares outstanding) to determine weighting. Since a stock's price

---

6. One potential candidate is the Rydex S&P Equal-weighted ETF (symbol: RSP) with an annual expense ratio of approximately 0.4 percent.

sometimes reflects the emotions of Mr. Market (which cause us to invest too much in expensive stocks and too little in bargain stocks), it's an advantage that none of these other measures of company size used in a fundamentally based index (like total sales, earnings, or book value) are affected by stock price at all.

The result of creating an index weighted by attributes that reflect economic footprint rather than market cap will still tend to weight the index toward larger companies. The benefit of weighting larger companies with greater amounts of sales, earnings, etc. more heavily is that fundamentally based indexes will end up owning businesses in proportions that are much more representative of the overall market and economy than equal weighting would provide. In many ways, this also makes more sense. If an industry such as oil has ten very large companies and another industry such as retail has forty-seven mostly smaller companies, an equally weighted index could put much more weight in retail than the relative size of the industry merits merely because it has a larger number of companies. Weighting by various measures of economic footprint avoids this problem.

Yet even though a fundamentally based index will concentrate more money in larger companies, it manages to avoid the systematic pricing flaws created by market cap weighting. It's very important to understand how. It's not that a fundamentally based index won't make mistakes. It will. Some of the companies that a fundamentally based index weights more heavily due to a large amount of sales, earnings, employees, or dividends will be overpriced by the market. Some companies with less sales or earnings than most may be underpriced and yet underweighted by a fundamental index. But these errors are not systematic. With a fundamentally based index, there will also be bargain-priced companies with large economic footprints that are weighted heavily in the index and overpriced smaller footprint companies that the fundamentally based index fortuitously assigns lower weightings.

In other words, because these weightings are not influenced by price at all, whatever pricing errors the market makes should, on average, cancel out over time. Basing weights on fundamental size won't make us extra money; it just won't systematically overweight the overpriced stocks and underweight the under-priced stocks like a market-cap-weighted index will. So in that sense, a fundamentally weighted index accomplishes a result similar to that of the equally weighted index. Instead of systematically overowning expensive stocks and underowning bargains like the market-cap-weighted index, both fundamental weight-ing and equal weighting distribute the market's pric-ing flaws randomly throughout the companies held in the index.

But fundamentally weighted indexes have a big advantage over simple equal weighting. Remember, the smallest stocks in an equally weighted index may not be very large. Yet because the money invested in the index must be distributed evenly, we have to invest as much money in the company with the smallest mar-ket capitalization as we do in the company with the largest market capitalization. So, as we've already dis-cussed, equal weighting can't handle large amounts of money (okay, it can probably handle tens of billions, but not hundreds of billions!).

On the other hand, a company's fundamental size often has a very high correlation with its market capital-ization. In other words, companies that have lots of sales and earnings usually have high market capitalizations. Companies with lower sales and earnings usually have lower market capitalizations. As a result, an index that uses fundamental weightings to determine how much to buy of each stock will tend to place more money in companies with larger market capitalizations and less money in companies with smaller market capitalizations. This makes it much easier for fundamentally weighted indexes to effectively handle larger amounts of money than it is for equally weighted indexes. In addition, since the fundamental characteristics of a company (such as sales, earnings, and book value) don't jump around like stock prices do, fundamental weightings don't change

ASSUME THE STOCK MARKET HAS ONLY THREE COMPANIES:

	MARKET CAPITALIZATION		LAST YEAR'S EARNINGS
Company A =	$6 billion		$100 million
Company B =	$3 billion		$300 million
Company C =	$1 billion		$200 million
Total Market Cap of All Companies	$10 billion	Total Earnings Of All Companies	$600 million

MARKET-CAP-WEIGHTED INDEX

$$\text{Company A} = \frac{\$6 \text{ billion}}{\$10 \text{ billion}} = 60\% \text{ weight in index}$$

$$\text{Company B} = \frac{\$3 \text{ billion}}{\$10 \text{ billion}} = 30\% \text{ weight in index}$$

$$\text{Company C} = \frac{\$1 \text{ billion}}{\$10 \text{ billion}} = 10\% \text{ weight in index}$$

The market-cap-weighted index, as the name implies, weights companies according to market cap. Here, Company A has a market capitalization of $6 billion, which is equal to 60% of the total market cap of all stocks ($10 billion).

EQUALLY WEIGHTED INDEX

Company A	=	33% weight in index
Company B	=	33% weight in index
Company C	=	33% weight in index

The equally weighted index weights all companies equally, regardless of size. Here, there are three companies in the stock universe, and therefore each gets a one-third weight in the index.

FUNDAMENTALLY WEIGHTED INDEX

Company B = $\dfrac{\$300\ \text{million}}{\$600\ \text{million}}$ = 50.0% weight in index

Company C = $\dfrac{\$200\ \text{million}}{\$600\ \text{million}}$ = 33.3% weight in index

Company A = $\dfrac{\$100\ \text{million}}{\$600\ \text{million}}$ = 16.7% weight in index

For the fundamentally weighted index, we used earnings as a measure of economic size. Earnings for the entire universe of companies equaled $600 million, so Company B, with $300 million in earnings, receives a weight of 50% in this fundamentally weighted index. Fundamentally weighted indexes often use additional measures of fundamental size such as cash flow, book value, sales, and/or dividends. Notice that market capitalization (and therefore market price) is not considered for this fundamental index.

all that drastically or often. So unlike equally weighted indexes that must reweight frequently along with changes in stock prices, not that much trading has to be done to keep the companies in the fundamentally weighted index at their proper weighting.

The bottom line is that fundamentally based indexes are probably a better option to replace market-cap-weighted indexes than are equally weighted indexes. The advantages are significant. In a fundamental index, company weightings are more representative of the overall economy than equally weighted indexes. Because larger companies usually have larger weights in a fundamental index, these indexes can handle much more money than equal weighting (which requires us to buy equal amounts of both large- and small-capitalization stocks). In addition, since company fundamentals don't change nearly as much as stock prices, fundamental indexes require much less trading than equally weighted indexes. But, of course, all of these advantages are wonderful only if fundamental indexes actually work. Fortunately, there's plenty of evidence that they do.

Although various methods of weighting portfolios by economic fundamentals have been around since the late 1980s, in recent years fundamental indexes researched and constructed by Research Affiliates and WisdomTree Investments have become some of the most popular and widely accessible. In fact, Rob Arnott and his team at Research Affiliates has backtested (and in recent years made available) an index that has outperformed the market-cap-weighted S&P 500 by approximately 2 percent per year since 1962 (before expenses).[7]

The Research Affiliates index (known as the FTSE RAFI 1000 Index) was constructed using a five-year average of company cash flows, sales, dividends, and book value. Companies were ranked and weighted based on a combination of these four characteristics of economic size, and the largest one thousand were purchased. Since market capitalization was not one of the factors used for weighting, some stocks selected for the RAFI index are a bit smaller than those stocks found in the Russell 1000; almost all stocks selected, however, should fall within the largest 1,200–1,400 stocks ranked by market capitalization. One reasonably cost-effective (annual expenses of 0.39–0.46 percent plus any trading commissions) and tax-efficient way to invest in this index is through an exchange-traded fund (ETF) listed on the New York Stock Exchange called PowerShares FTSE RAFI US 1000 Portfolio (symbol: PRF).[8] In addition, RAFI has created other fundamentally weighted equity indexes for

---

7. See Robert Arnott, Jason Hsu, and Philip Moore, "Fundamental Indexation," *Financial Analysts Journal*, March/April, 2005.

8. Many ETFs are treated in a similar way from a tax perspective to the way a stock purchase and sale are treated. Any profits would generally be taxed at long-term capital gains rates for ETFs held for longer than one year (dividends would still be taxed at the prevailing rate for dividends).

smaller-capitalization stocks and for certain international markets.[9]

While fundamentally weighted indexes have some clear advantages over equally weighted indexes, both provide an attractive option for investors when compared to capitalization-weighted indexes such as the S&P 500 and the Russell 1000. Since, over time, capitalization-weighted indexes seem to beat the vast majority of active managers, that's really saying something!

Then again, I think we can do better. Let's see how.

SUMMARY

1. Over time, most professional managers can't beat market-capitalization-weighted indexes such as the S&P 500 or the Russell 1000.

2. If Mr. Market sometimes prices stocks based on emotion, market-capitalization-weighted indexes will systematically buy too much of the overpriced stocks and too little of the bargain-priced stocks.

---

9. WisdomTree, similarly, has created fundamentally weighted ETFs using various measures of dividends and earnings.

3. Equally weighted indexes won't do this.

4. Fundamentally weighted indexes won't, either. Plus they have some practical advantages over equally weighted indexes.

5. But I think we can do better.

6. So how do you keep an idiot in suspense?[10]

---

10. I'll tell you later! (Just kidding!)

CHAPTER
EIGHT

So I'm running along in this five-mile race for charity. The distance is a little longer and I'm moving a little faster than I'm used to, but all in all, I'm doing fine. Around mile four, though, I'm starting to get a bit tired when I see what can only be described as a pretty sad sight. There he is, this disheveled-looking older gentleman in a sleeveless undershirt, probably in his late sixties and at least thirty or forty pounds north of out-of-shape, slapping his feet against the pavement in ducklike fashion. But that's not the whole picture. He's coughing and wheezing nonstop, like the longtime smoker that he probably is, and each stride is so labored and at such an awkward rhythm that it's not really clear exactly when, or if, the next step is coming.

That's when I realize. He's ahead of me! I'm not sure if beating him out at the finish line by a good twenty yards counts as just a great wake-up call or one of the most humbling moments of my life, but whatever I took from the experience, at least my private humiliation was all for charity. But I kind of feel that last chapter was a little like my experience with that other runner. I can say or think what I want about the flaws and shortcomings of investing in market-cap-weighted indexes, but for most investors, they've still been pretty tough to beat. Now that investors have been provided with some easily accessible and perhaps superior options such as equally weighted and any number of fundamentally weighted indexes, I think they have a good chance to eke out a victory over time. Actually, *eke* might be the wrong word because earning an extra 1 to 1.5 percent each year after expenses can still add up over the long term.[1] But just so I have a chance to redeem what little pride I have left, why don't we see if there's possibly some other way to beat out a guy in a sleeveless undershirt.

Last chapter, we learned about Mr. Market. Mr. Market, as you recall, is very emotional at times, and as a result, over the shorter term (which can still last

---

1. Earning 9.5 percent per year versus 8 percent over twenty years, for instance, yields a 32 percent larger nest egg.

several years), markets can overreact by pricing certain stocks either too high or too low. If our goal is to buy bargain-priced stocks (stocks priced below fair value), we should probably see if we can figure out a systematic way to take advantage of Mr. Market when he is being too pessimistic.

One way to do this is to buy a group of stocks that the market is not willing to pay a lot for. In Chapter 4, we learned about the concept of earnings yield. If you recall, we expected Candy's Candies to earn $10,000 next year. The purchase price for the entire Candy's Candies business was $100,000. So paying $100,000 for a business that earns $10,000 each year would give us an earnings yield of 10 percent ($10,000 ÷ $100,000 = 10%). If earnings were $12,000 instead, the earnings yield would be 12 percent. All things being equal, if we're going to pay $100,000 for a business, we'd rather it earn us 12 percent a year rather than 10 percent. In other words, we'd rather get more earnings relative to the price we are paying, rather than less. So let's work with that concept.

Next year's earnings are always uncertain. However, last year's earnings are already known. One way to compare companies without having to make guesses about the future is to look at their earnings yields based on last year's earnings. We could just rank all companies against one another using last year's earnings and compare those earnings to the current price for each company. The companies with higher earnings yields would be ranked toward the top and the companies with lower earnings yields would be ranked toward the bottom (or another way to think about it—the companies that earned a lot relative to the price we are paying rank higher than the companies that earn less relative to the price we are paying).

Let's analyze that for a minute. Why would the market allow us to buy some companies at a price that gives us a 15 percent earnings yield based on last year's earnings while others are priced to give us only a 5 percent earnings yield? Well, to help understand why, we can use some of what we learned a bit earlier. The most obvious point is that when we last looked at earnings yield, we were trying to figure out what our earnings yield would be based on future earnings. In this case, I just suggested using last year's earnings to calculate our earnings yield. As we've already learned, since the value of the business comes from what it will earn for us going forward, there is no guarantee that next year's earnings will be as high as last year's. A company that has a 15 percent earnings yield based on last year's earnings may have a lower earnings yield going forward if earnings decline in coming years. A company with a 5 percent earnings yield based on last year's earnings could have a higher earnings yield going forward if earnings grow over coming years.

In fact, this is probably what the market is expecting! That's why it is letting us earn 15 percent (based on last year's earnings) when we buy one company and only 5 percent (again, based on last year's earnings) when we buy another. For many of the companies with very high earnings yields based on last year's earnings, the market price is reflecting expectations that future earnings may not be so great. There is probably a concern that earnings going forward may either grow very slowly or actually decline. For companies with low earnings yields based on last year's earnings, expectations are probably the opposite. The high market price relative to last year's earnings is usually reflecting expectations of higher earnings and high growth going forward.

But here's the thing. Mr. Market often overreacts. Companies where there are low expectations are often sold down to prices that are too low. Companies where there are high expectations are often pushed to prices that may be too high. So when we buy companies with high earnings yields based on last year's earnings, we are probably buying a lot of companies where expectations for next year are pretty low. Hopefully, due to an emotional Mr. Market, some of these companies may have been sold down by too much. After all, who wants to own a company where the expected earnings for next year or the year after don't look so great?

So here's the plan. Instead of weighting companies by how big they are based on either market capitalization (like market-cap-weighted indexes) or economic footprint (like fundamentally weighted indexes), let's weight them by how cheap they appear. In our case, we're going to look at how cheaply we can buy a company relative to its last year of earnings. But weighting companies based on how cheap they appear relative to sales, book value, an average of the last several years of earnings, or other factors would also be perfectly valid methods. For what we'll call our *value-weighted index*, the cheaper a company appears, the more we'll own of it. In this way, maybe we'll be able to create an index that is systematically overweighted in companies where expectations are low and where there is a good possibility that an emotional Mr. Market has sold the shares down to bargain levels. But before we move forward, let's first see if we can improve a bit on our value-weighted index.

As we've already learned, Benjamin Graham's focus was on buying companies at prices well below fair value. By buying companies at a bargain price, he could invest with a large margin of safety. But his most famous student, Warren Buffett, went even one step further. Buffett (influenced strongly by his partner, Charlie Munger) added a particularly powerful concept to Graham's teachings that is probably a major reason why Buffett has become one of the world's most successful investors. Simply stated, Buffett suggested that while buying a business at a bargain price is great, buying a *good* business at a bargain price is even better.

So before we create our own value-weighted index, we should probably figure out a way to take advantage of this important insight. While there are clearly many ways to define what makes a business *good,* the measure we're going to use is easy to calculate and has the added benefit that you already know what it is! Just as when we invest our own money we would prefer to receive a high rate of return (a high earnings yield) rather than a low one, likewise, we want to find businesses that can invest their own money at high rates of return also.

In the case of Candy's Candies, we would obviously rather buy the business at a price where we expect to receive a 20 percent earnings yield rather than a 10 percent earnings yield. Similarly, when Candy's Candies decides to invest some of its own earnings in a new store, it would like to receive a 20 percent annual return on that investment rather than a 10 percent return.

Companies that can expand by investing some or all of their earnings at very high rates of return are generally much more attractive than companies that can only re-invest earnings at much lower rates of return.

Essentially, a business needs two things in order to operate: *working capital* and *fixed assets.* So when Candy's Candies decides to open a new store, the working capital needed in the new store would include enough money to buy its inventory of candy. Its fixed assets would include the cost of building the new store and store displays. Our goal is simply to measure how well Candy's Candies (or any company) can turn new investments in working capital and fixed assets into earnings.

Clearly, a company that can earn $20,000 each year from a new store that requires $50,000 worth of working capital and fixed assets to open sounds pretty good. That would equal what is known as a 40 percent *return on capital* ($20,000 ÷ $50,000 = 40%). Few investors or businesses have the opportunity to invest money at such high rates of return. On the other hand, a company that earns $5,000 on a new store that also requires a $50,000 initial investment is earning only a 10 percent return on capital. For our purposes, we will assume a company that can earn 40 percent returns on new investments is in a better business than one that can earn only 10 percent on new investments.

Of course, since we're still talking about the future, we don't really know for sure what return a business will earn on its investment in a new store or a new factory. But we *can* look at what kind of return the business has achieved in the past. By comparing last year's earnings to the amount of working capital and fixed assets already in the business (information found on every company balance sheet), we can often get a good idea of what future returns on capital will be like. So once again, if one company earned a 40 percent return on capital last year and another only 10 percent, we will assume that the one that earned 40 percent is in the better business.[2]

Now, back to our value-weighted index! What would happen if we constructed an index that weighted stocks not based on size but based on a combination of how "cheap" and "good" they were? What if, similar to a fundamental index, we chose roughly 800–1000 companies (from the largest 1,400 companies as measured by market capitalization)? What if we compared the historical results over the last several decades to market-cap-weighted indexes like the Russell 1000 or the S&P 500? How would we do?

---

2. Shameless tout: For a fuller explanation of the concepts behind *earnings yield* and *return on capital*, feel free to read *The Little Book That Still Beats the Market* (by Joel Greenblatt).

YEAR	VALUE-WEIGHTED INDEX	RUSSELL 1000	S&P 500
1990	(8.8)%	(4.2)%	(3.1)%
1991	48.7	33.0	30.5
1992	19.2	8.9	7.6
1993	16.3	10.2	10.1
1994	4.2	0.4	1.3
1995	38.8	37.8	37.6
1996	23.4	22.4	23.0
1997	33.0	32.9	33.4
1998	9.1	27.0	28.6
1999	8.6	20.9	21.0
2000	18.7	(7.8)	(9.1)
2001	15.3	(12.4)	(11.9)
2002	(6.7)	(21.7)	(22.1)
2003	40.7	29.9	28.7
2004	21.5	11.4	10.9
2005	10.3	6.3	4.9
2006	17.5	15.5	15.8
2007	2.7	5.8	5.5
2008	(35.3)	(37.6)	(37.0)
2009	48.5	28.4	26.5
2010 (6 mos.)	(2.0)	(6.4)	(6.7)
Compounded Return	**13.9%**[3]	**7.9%**	**7.6%**

3. After modeled costs of trading and market impact. Data source: CompuStat point-in-time database. Value-weighted Index versus Russell 1000 during test period: Beta = 1.0; Upside capture = 116%; Downside capture = 89%; Sharpe ratio = .61 versus .27; Sortino = .91 versus .38; Information ratio = .85.

Of course, as already mentioned, we don't really have to use a combination of earnings yield and return on capital to create our value-weighted index. There are other well-established measures of cheapness that have a good historical record and could be used to create alternative value-weighted indexes.[4] In fact, there are already a number of ways to invest in widely diversified funds that combine some of these other "value" measures with a mechanical or highly systematic approach to creating stock portfolios.[5] Also, there are additional value-oriented factors that we have found over the years that have worked even better than the ones used in our test. It's just that using the logical concepts we've just examined, earnings yield and return on capital, works really well!

For nontaxable accounts, earning 13.9 percent on an annualized basis turns $1 at the beginning of the test period into approximately $14.41 at the end.[6] For

---

4. These could include variants of price-to-earnings, price-to-cash-flow, price-to-dividends, price-to-book, price-to-sales, or any number of other measures of potential cheapness.

5. See appendix.

6. Even after subtracting typical mutual fund expenses (1.25 percent per year), returns would have approximated 12.65 percent per year and turned $1 into $11.50 during the test period in a nontaxable account.

the Russell 1000 during that same period at a 7.9 percent annualized return, $1 would turn to $4.75. That's a big difference!

So now you know. But is that really the big secret?

SUMMARY

1. Market-cap-weighted indexes beat most active managers.

2. Equally weighted indexes and fundamentally weighted indexes beat market-cap-weighted indexes.

3. *Value-weighted* indexes can beat them all!

4. But is that really the big secret?

5. NO! (The big secret is that guy almost beat me!)

FOR ADVANCED STUDENTS AND THE MERELY SKEPTICAL

Is our value-weighted index really an index? Is it an active strategy? Is it just the value effect? Is it just the small-cap effect?

Our index portfolio consists of 800–1,000 companies selected from the largest 1,400 companies based on market capitalization. As opposed to using market capitalization, equal weighting, or a fundamental measure of economic size to establish company weights for a 500–1,000 stock portfolio, the value-weighted index uses measures of "cheapness" (trailing earnings yield) and "quality" (trailing return on capital). In this sense, a value-weighted index is constructed in a fashion similar to other indexes.

Market-cap-weighted indexes such as the S&P 500 and the Russell 1000 are very low turnover portfolios because market caps adjust automatically with stock prices. Annual turnover for these market-cap-weighted indexes are approximately 6–8 percent per year (i.e., for every $100 invested, approximately $6–$8 must be traded each year to keep the index in balance with changes in market capitalizations and special corporate events like mergers and bankruptcies). A fundamental index such as the RAFI Index of 1,000 large-cap U.S. stocks is also a very low turnover index. This is because company fundamentals based on economic size, like sales, book value, cash flows, and dividends, do not often change significantly within a year's time. This type of fundamental index may turn over at a rate of 10-12 percent each year. Equally weighted indexes may turn over at a rate of 16-20 percent per year depending upon how frequently they are rebalanced.

On the other hand, the average actively managed equity mutual fund portfolio turns over approximately 100 percent or more each year. In this sense, our value-weighted index looks much more like an actively managed portfolio. As the portfolio is continually rebalanced toward the stocks that rank highest based on measures of "cheapness" and "quality," turnover averaged approximately 80-100 percent per year during the period tested. (Note: Trading costs and market impact were modeled, and the returns listed for our value-weighted index are net returns after subtracting our estimates for these costs and impact.)

As for diversification, the value-weighted index looks much more like a widely diversified index. As already mentioned, the top twenty stocks in the S&P 500 can account for approximately 33 percent of the value of the entire index. The top twenty stocks in our value-weighted index usually account for just over 6 percent of the entire portfolio. Although the Russell 1000 index contains the largest one thousand U.S.-based stocks based on market capitalization, because the index is so heavily weighted toward the largest companies, the level of diversification for the index is equivalent to owning a portfolio of approximately 175–200 equally weighted stocks. That's a lot of diversification. But using that same measure of diversification, our value-weighted index is roughly equivalent to owning an equally weighted portfolio of more than 500 stocks. In this sense, too, the value-weighted portfolio is obviously more similar to an index than to most actively managed portfolios. (Interestingly, over the test period, the overlap in holdings [on a dollar-invested basis] between our value-weighted index and the Russell 1000 averaged only approximately 33 percent.)

Of course, the value-weighted index takes advantage of the well-known value effect. Companies that appear cheap relative to earnings, cash flows, dividends, book value, and sales have historically been shown to beat the major market indexes such as the S&P 500 and the Russell 1000 by as much as 2–3 percent per year over long periods of time. This outperformance is often bumpy, and value stocks can, and often do, underperform for years at a time.

However, it appears that some of the recorded value effect is due to using a somewhat flawed benchmark. As already discussed, if we assume that market prices often reflect emotions rather than value, market-cap-weighted indexes will tend to systematically buy too much of the overpriced stocks and too little of the underpriced stocks. Performance improvements from simply randomly weighting these errors through equally weighting or fundamentally weighting portfolios may indicate that 1–2 percent of the value advantage may merely be a result of correcting for some of the systematic flaws inherent in the market-cap-weighting methodology. Obviously, our value-weighted index also benefits from this effect in comparisons with market-cap-weighted indexes.

What about the small-cap effect? Does the value-weighted portfolio outperform partially because other indexes are biased toward larger-cap stocks? Both the market-cap-weighted index (by definition) and the fundamental index (due to a high correlation between economic size and market cap) are clearly tilted toward larger-market-capitalization stocks. Since it is widely believed that small-cap stocks outperform large-cap stocks over time, does this account for some of the outperformance of the value-weighted index?

In short, the answer is no. The Russell 1000 index consists of the largest one thousand U.S.-based stocks ranked by market capitalization. The Russell 2000 index includes stocks 1,001–3,000 ranked by market capitalization. Over the last thirty years, since the inception of the Russell 1000 and Russell 2000 indexes (including our test period), returns for the two indexes have been almost identical, just several basis points apart.

At this writing, the smallest stock in the Russell 2000 has a market capitalization of approximately $150 million. Most studies that have found a small-cap effect prior to the last thirty years found this effect in stocks that were significantly smaller than the smallest stock in the Russell 2000 (i.e., stocks with significantly smaller market capitalizations than the 3000th largest stock). Therefore, this research was never meant to apply to the universe of stocks used in our study (the largest 1,400 stocks by market capitalization).[7] In addition, our research into trading costs, bid-ask spreads, and market impact make us strongly suspect that the small-cap effect found in these earlier studies is unlikely to be real. In other words, the small-cap effect would largely disappear in the real world due to the lack of liquidity and high trading costs for these smaller companies.

---

7. See Edward F. McQuarrie, "The Chimera of Small Stock Outperformance," *Journal of Investing*, Fall 2010.

Nevertheless, investing in small stocks still has some major advantages over investing in larger-cap companies. These stocks, because of their smaller size, are subject to less research from both institutional and individual investors. Consequently, they are often more likely to be mispriced by the market than larger capitalization stocks. This means they can often be priced either too high or too low. As a result, smaller-capitalization stocks may provide more opportunity for enterprising investors even if, on average as a group, they do not outperform stocks with larger market capitalizations.

CHAPTER
NINE

There's a scene in one of the great movies of all time, *The Sting*, where Robert Redford and Paul Newman play two con men in the 1930s plotting to take on a major Chicago mob boss to avenge the death of their friend. Newman plays the experienced old pro, and Redford, the impetuous con artist in training. So in this scene, we see both con men surveying the crime boss from a safe distance. We watch the cocky Redford, from his hiding place behind a newspaper, turn to Newman and scoff in the gangster's direction, "He's not as tough as he thinks."

Newman, the old hand, leans in and deadpans, "Neither are we."

Well, when it comes to investing, Newman's voice of experience might as well be talking directly to us. There's actually a whole school of investment thought, known as *behavioral finance*, which pretty much concludes that we're not tough at all. In fact, just the opposite. While entire books have been written on the topic, the bottom line is pretty simple: we're practically hardwired from birth to be lousy investors.

Our survival instincts make us fear loss much more than we enjoy gain. Just like on the savannas in Africa, we run from danger first and ask questions later. No wonder we panic out of our investments when things look bleakest—we're just trying to survive! We have a herd mentality that makes us feel more comfortable staying with the pack. So buying high when everyone else is buying and selling low when everyone else is selling comes quite naturally—it just makes us feel better! We use our primitive instincts to make quick decisions based on limited data, and we weight most heavily what has just happened. Given the shortcuts that worked for us in the wild, of course we run from managers who performed poorly most recently and into the arms of last year's winners—that just seems like the right thing to do! And I'm sure having a strong ego must have had some benefits over time, too, so as a result, we all think we're above average! That's probably why we consistently overestimate our ability to pick good stocks or to find above-average managers. It's also this outsized ego that likely gives us the confidence to keep trading too much. And maybe that's why we keep making the same investing mistakes over and over—we just figure this time we'll get it right!

Understanding some of these things about ourselves is actually pretty powerful. It's from this understanding of our natural responses that we can begin to explain things like the most recent bubbles in housing and the Internet. To a large extent, maybe the value effect we examined in the last chapter is merely a result of the emotional overreactions that are built into all of us. Maybe it helps explain why Mr. Market acts crazy at times. But maybe it's also why we can't seem to take advantage of Mr. Market's craziness just when we should. Then again, none of this is really our fault! After all, we're busy surviving, herding, fixating on what just happened, and being overconfident!

So how do I propose we deal with all these primitive emotions and lousy investing instincts? My answer is really quite simple: we don't! Let's just give up before we start! Let's admit that we'll probably keep making the same investing mistakes no matter how many books on behavioral investing we read. Next time that lion comes charging toward us, let's just assume we're going to run!

So now what?

Here's the plan. Let's take advantage of the fact that everyone else is human, too. Let's develop a strategy that helps keep us from making *our* mistakes. But at the same time, let's assume that everybody else will keep making *theirs*! Maybe we can find some systematic way to save us from ourselves by tying our hands behind our backs ahead of time. But ideally, our plan should also leave us with enough rope to beat the market and almost all other investors!

How are we going to do all that? Well, we already have part of the solution. Clearly, we should start with a strategy that should outperform most others over time. As we've already learned, a market-cap-weighted index fund will likely outperform most active managers. Of course, over time, an equally weighted index fund or a fundamentally weighted index fund should do even better. But as we saw in the last chapter, a value-weighted index should do better still—and possibly by a lot! And if we choose the value-weighted index fund, we'll actually be taking advantage of the systematic mistakes that most of us humans make, rather than suffering from them!

Remember, the only reason the value strategy works is that we are systematically setting ourselves up to buy companies that most people don't want. For many of the companies that the value-weighted index favors, next year or the year after doesn't look so good. In general, our emotions tell us to shy away from these. On the other hand, everyone already knows the bad news, and on average we don't have to pay a lot for our purchases. In fact, on average, people overreact and we get to own a portfolio filled with bargains! The important thing is that we do this systematically. By buying a diversified portfolio based on just the numbers, not emotions, we've taken our first step.

But here's the big problem. While our value strategy makes sense and seems to work over long periods of time, unfortunately, it doesn't always work. In Chapter 6 we learned that if you follow a strategy that differs from market-cap-weighted indexes like the S&P 500 or the Russell 1000, there can be long periods of underperformance. Even the best-performing managers over a recent decade (the top 25 percent of active managers over a ten-year period) spent many years during the decade as the worst performers. In fact, almost half of these successful managers spent at least three years in the bottom 10 percent! Similarly, our value-weighted index has spent years at a time underperforming the major indexes. It's just that over longer periods of time, it works incredibly well.

On the other hand, we're probably pretty lucky that our value strategy doesn't always work. If it worked every month and every year, everyone would buy the value-weighted index and eventually it would stop working! But that just brings up our other problem.

Sure, we have a plan that works over the long term, but we're only human. After a year or two of underperformance, our instincts will tell us to run! Forget underperformance—after a year or two of losses, whether or not we outperform the market, we're going to run too! It's nothing personal. It's not even our fault. It's just in our nature! We've already decided that!

Luckily, *"Part B"* of our plan is designed just for us humans (though other species are free to keep reading). But before we get there, we have to step back for a minute and take another look at what we're trying to accomplish in the first place.

This whole book has been a discussion of how to invest in the stock market. Traditionally, stocks have provided high returns and have been a mainstay of most investors' portfolios. Since a share of stock merely represents an ownership interest in an actual business, owning a portfolio of stocks just means we're entitled to a share in the future income of all those businesses. If we can buy good businesses that grow over time and we can buy them at bargain prices, this should continue to be a good way to invest a portion of our savings over the long term. Following a similar strategy with international stocks (companies based outside of the United States) for some of our savings would also seem to make sense (in this way, we could own businesses whose profits might not be as dependent on the U.S. economy or the U.S. currency).

But let me repeat: this whole book has been a discussion of how to invest in the stock market—and only the stock market! That's it. For the portion of our money that we choose to invest in the stock market, we now should have a better idea of how company valuation is supposed to work, of how Wall Street professionals should work (but don't), and of how we can outperform the major market averages and most other investors. That's a big deal! We now have a great plan for how to invest in the stock market! What we don't have is a plan for *how much* to invest in the stock market in the first place.

So here's the deal. Despite the last decade's poor returns for the broad market as represented by the major market-cap-weighted indexes (and including the knowledge that we can instead buy a value-weighted index that would have done quite well during this same period), I firmly believe that it makes sense for almost everyone to have a significant portion of their assets in stocks. But just as important, few people should put *all* their money in stocks. Whether you choose to invest 80 percent of your savings in stocks or 40 percent in stocks depends in part on individual circumstances and in part on how human you really are.

An investment strategy where 100 percent of your assets are invested in the stock market can result in a drop of 30 percent, 40 percent, or even more in your net worth in any given year (of course, many people learned this the hard way in recent years).[1] Since most of us are only human, we can't take a drop of this size without opting for survival. That means either panicking out or being forced to sell at just the wrong time. In fact, if we start with the premise that we can't handle a 40 percent drop, then putting 100 percent of our money in the stock market is a strategy that is almost guaranteed to fail at some inopportune time down the road.

Obviously, if we invest only 50 percent of our assets in stocks, a market drop of 40 percent would result in losing "only" 20 percent of our net worth.[2] As painful as this still might be, if we maintain the proper long-term perspective, some of us might be better able to withstand a drop of this size without running for our lives. So it really comes down to this. Whether you choose to place 80 percent of your assets in stocks or 40 percent, that percentage should be based largely on

---

1. Losses of this size can occur even with no borrowing through a margin account.

2. Though it depends where we have the rest of our assets at the time!

how much pain you can take on the downside and still hang in there. And *now* we're finally ready for "Part B" of our plan!

Pick a number. What percentage of your assets do you feel comfortable investing in stocks? The important thing is to choose a portion of your assets to invest in the stock market—and stick with it! For most people, this number could be between 40 percent and 80 percent of investable assets, but each case is too individual to give a range that works for everyone. Whatever number you do choose, though, I can guarantee one thing: at some point you will regret your decision.

Being only human, when the market goes down you will regret putting so much into stocks. And if the value-weighted index goes down more than the market, you'll regret it even more! If the market goes up, the opposite will happen—you'll wonder why you were such a chicken in the first place. And at some point, if the popular market indexes outperform the value-weighted strategy for long enough, you'll wonder why you listened to me at all! That's just the way it is. (Actually, according to behavioral finance theory, that's just the way *you* is!)

So here's what we're going to do. Against my better judgment, we're going to give you some rope to play with. Once you pick your number, let's say 60 percent in stocks, you can adjust your exposure up or down by 10 percent whenever you want. So you can go down to 50 percent invested in stocks and up to 70 percent, but that's it.[3] You can't sell everything when things go against you, and you can't jump in with both feet and invest 100 percent when everything is rocking and rolling your way. It's not allowed! (In any event, doing this would put you in serious violation of Part B of our plan!)[4]

And here's the big secret: if you actually follow our plan, small investors will have a huge advantage over professionals—an advantage that has only been growing larger every year. Of course, you would think that with all the newly minted MBAs heading to Wall Street each year, the proliferation of giant hedge funds over the last few decades, the growth of professionally managed mutual funds and ETFs, the increasingly widespread availability of instant news and timely company information, and the mushrooming ability to crunch massive amounts of company and economic data at an affordable price, the competition to beat the market

---

3. Please limit yourself to at most one round trip up and/or down a year or less!

4. The consequences of which are just too unspeakable to mention. Trust me.

would actually be growing fiercer with each passing year. And in some ways it is. But in one important way, perhaps *the* most important, the competition is actually getting easier.

The truth is that it's really hard to be a professional stock market investor today. The march of technology has made it easy for clients to monitor returns, and in many cases to scrutinize investment positions on a daily basis. The lucky managers, the ones who have clients with a "long term" perspective, get to report results on a monthly basis. Since most clients can only evaluate performance results (rather than the quality of the work that went into each investment decision), there have been a million ways developed over the last few decades to slice and dice these performance data into all kinds of ratios and statistics.

The only thing is that evaluating past performance data for even a several-year period may be unhelpful when it comes to predicting future success. Yet almost all hire-and-fire decisions made by clients (both individual and professional) are based on a manager's performance during the last couple of years. While this is perhaps understandable, it forces most managers to concentrate on short-term performance. As we've already discussed, even if a manager has a healthy long-term perspective and is willing to wait out short-term underperformance, most *clients* are not! After two years of underperformance, or three years at the most, most clients leave. Just as important, after two or three years of underperformance, there is almost zero chance of getting new clients. Under those circumstances, what's a manager to do?

In the late 1980s, I had just signed up a new client for our investment partnership. This client was one of the first investment firms known as a *fund-of-funds*. These are professional investors who collect money from clients but do not manage the money themselves. Instead, the managers of the fund-of-funds use their expertise to select a group of "good" managers and invest the money with them. At the time, I was providing performance information to my clients on a quarterly basis. At the request of my new client, I agreed to provide the fund-of-funds with performance returns each month.

Sure enough, after one month our partnership was up 1.1 percent. Not bad, except that our new fund-of-funds client called and informed us that other similar partnerships in which they had invested had been up an average of 1.2 percent during the same period. To what did I attribute our "underperformance"? (No, I'm not kidding.) As politely as I could, I suggested that perhaps they should call me back in a year. Of course, if I had responded that a more meaningful period over which to evaluate our performance would probably be four or five years, that would have been closer to the truth. Then again, I'm pretty sure that bit of investment wisdom would have been met with a suggestion to "be fruitful and multiply" (but, as Woody Allen would say, not exactly in those words).

Well, institutional investors dominate the stock market even more today than they did twenty years ago. The practice of providing daily or monthly information and analysis on investment performance is standard operating procedure. Everyone does it. It's expected, and in most cases it's required. Today there's absolutely no chance that any fund-of-funds would graciously agree to call back in a year. In fact, investment fiduciaries, such as the managers of pension funds, endowments, insurance companies, and fund-of-funds, would be considered negligent if they didn't continually monitor and actively analyze the activities and performance of the fund managers to whom they allocated client assets.[5] This is completely understandable. As a fiduciary myself in several situations, I need to do it, too.

---

5. Investment fiduciaries are those charged with the legal obligation to look out for the interests of their investment clients.

It's just that it's really hard to look at returns every day and every month, to receive analysis every month or every quarter, and still keep a long-term perspective. Most individual and institutional investors can't do it. They can't help analyzing the short-term information they do have, even if it's relatively meaningless over the long term. On the bright side, as the market has become more institutionalized and performance information and statistics have become more ubiquitous, the advantages for those who can maintain a long-term perspective have only grown.

For those investing in individual stocks, the benefits to looking past the next quarter or the next year, to investing in companies that may take several years before they can show good results, to truly taking a long-term perspective when evaluating a stock investment remain as large, if not larger, than they have ever been.[6] Remember from early in our journey, the value of a business comes from all the cash earnings we expect to collect from that business over its lifetime. Earnings from the next few years are usually only a very small portion of this value. Yet most investment professionals, stuck in an environment where short-term perfor-

---

6. The advantage that comes from looking past the next several years and focusing on long-term value while nearly everyone else focuses on near-term issues is sometimes referred to as *time arbitrage*.

mance is a real concern, often feel forced to focus on short-term business and economic issues rather than on long-term value. This is great news and a growing advantage for individual and professional investors who can truly maintain a long-term investment perspective.

Luckily, since it's particularly hard for most non-professionals to calculate values for individual stocks, this focus on the short term by professionals is also a huge advantage for individual investors who follow an intelligently and logically designed strategy like our value-weighted index. Because value strategies often *don't* work over shorter time frames, institutional pressures and individual instincts will continue to make it difficult for most investors to stick with them over the long term. For these investors, several years is simply too long to wait.

That's why "Part B" of our plan is so important. Hanging in there will be tough for us, too. But as individual investors, we have some major advantages over the large institutions. We don't have to answer to clients. We don't have to provide daily or monthly returns. We don't have to worry about staying in business. We just have to set up rules ahead of time that help us stay with our plan over the long term. We have to choose an allocation to stocks that is appropriate for our individual circumstances and then stick with it. When we feel like panicking after a large market drop or ditching our value-weighted strategy after a period of underperformance, we can—but only within our preset limits. When things are going great and we want to buy more, no problem, we can—we just can't buy too much. "Part B" of our plan won't let us!

So there it is. We have a strategy that beats the market. We have a plan that will help us hang in there. And, as individual investors, we have some major advantages over the investment professionals. All we need now is a little more encouragement. Perhaps a final visit with Benjamin Graham will help push us on our way.

In an interview shortly before he passed away, Graham provided us with these words of wisdom:

> The main point is to have the right general principles and the character to stick to them. . . . The thing that I have been emphasizing in my own work for the last few years has been the group approach. To try to buy groups of stocks that meet some simple criterion for being undervalued—regardless of the industry and with very little attention to the individual company. . . . Imagine—there seems to be practically

a foolproof way of getting good results out of common stock investment with a minimum of work. It seems too good to be true. But all I can tell you after 60 years of experience, it seems to stand up under any of the tests that I would make up.[7]

That interview took place thirty-five years ago. Yet we still have an opportunity to benefit from Graham's sage advice today.

I wish you all—the patience to succeed and the time to enjoy it. Good luck.

---

7. "An Hour with Benjamin Graham," *Financial Analysts Journal*, November/December 1976.

APPENDIX

Here are my suggestions for the most effective ways to immediately take advantage of the lessons found in *The Big Secret for the Small Investor.*

First, for taxable accounts, I have a strong preference for a special kind of closed-end mutual fund known as an *ETF* (or exchange-traded fund). These investment funds trade on stock exchanges and can be bought and sold in the same way that you would buy or sell a normal stock. Most ETFs are constructed to track an index such as the S&P 500, Russell 1000, or other more specialized indexes (these can be indexes for smaller stocks, specific industry groups, or even bonds and commodities).

The big advantage for ETFs, besides relatively low costs and ease of trading (in most cases), is taxes. In general, most capital gains taxes are realized only upon the sale of an ETF investment. So ETFs that are held for more than a year and show a profit will receive long-term capital gains treatment upon sale. (At this writing, long-term capital gains rates are significantly lower than the short-term capital gains rates that apply to capital assets held for less than one year.)

In other words, if you hold a particular ETF for two years, regardless of how much short-term trading takes place in the underlying stock portfolio of the fund during those two years, in many cases you would receive long-term capital gains treatment on most of your gain only upon sale of the ETF. (Dividends that are received during the holding period, however, would be taxed at the prevailing dividend tax rate at the time of the dividend.) For regular mutual funds that are not ETFs, this is not the case. For the typical mutual fund, taxes are paid by mutual fund holders based upon the trading of the underlying portfolio and are not deferred until the time of redemption. In short, with many ETFs, you don't pay most of your capital gains taxes until you sell the ETF. This can result in a lower overall tax rate and deferral of most capital gain tax liabilities for the entire holding period.

The disadvantage of ETFs is that most active managers who believe they can add value over time do not like to disclose their stock holdings on a daily basis (which is a requirement for ETFs). This would make their research efforts too easy to copy and perhaps dissipate their excess returns over time. Mutual funds are only required to disclose their holdings on a quarterly basis.

So here are my ETF and mutual fund suggestions:

EQUALLY WEIGHTED ETF

Rydex S&P Equal Weight ETF (symbol: RSP)

This is an equally weighted index of the S&P 500 that over time has outperformed the market-cap-weighted S&P 500 by approximately 1–2 percent per year. Price and value criteria are not included in this index.

FUNDAMENTALLY WEIGHTED ETF

PowerShares FTSE RAFI US 1000 (symbol: PRF)

This is a fundamentally weighted index based on economic size (rather than market cap). Economic size is measured based on five-year averages of book value, cash flow, dividends, and sales. This is the index designed by Research Affiliates. This ETF, based upon past history, can be expected to outperform the Russell 1000 or S&P 500 index by approximately 1–2 percent per year after expenses. Price and value criteria are not included in this index.

VALUE INDEX ETFS (NOT "VALUE-WEIGHTED")

These ETFs are based on various value indexes as constructed by either Russell or Vanguard. For example, the Russell 1000 Value Index selects a subgroup of companies from the Russell 1000 stock universe that have certain value characteristics. Generally, the stocks in the value index appear cheap relative to earnings, book value, and/or other similar measures. This subgroup of value stocks (approximately 650 stocks) is then weighted by market capitalization. In other words, the stocks selected for the value index are the "cheapest" portion of the Russell 1000 index, but the individual stocks in the value index are not weighted by how cheap they are. They are still weighted by market capitalization. In that sense, it is not a true value-weighted index. However, these ETFs should still take advantage of the long-term benefits of investing in stocks with certain simple value characteristics. They also achieve the tax benefits of an ETF. A reasonable expectation for outperformance over market-cap-weighted indexes is approximately 2 percent per year over the very long term.

iShares Russell 1000 Value Index Fund (symbol: IWD)—larger stocks

iShares Russell 2000 Value Index Fund (symbol: IWN)—smaller stocks

iShares Russell Midcap Value Index Fund (symbol: IWS)

iShares Russell Small Cap Value Index Fund (symbol: IJS)

Vanguard Value ETF (symbol: VTV)

Vanguard Mid-Cap Value Index Fund (symbol: VOE)

Vanguard Small-Cap Value ETF: (symbol: VBR)

INTERNATIONAL VALUE INDEX ETF

iShares MSCI EAFE Value Index Fund (symbol: EFV)—based on EAFE International Value Index

MUTUAL FUNDS ("VALUE-WEIGHTED")

We have created a free website, *valueweightedindex. com,* to keep readers updated on what I believe will be a growing area in the investment field. In addition to value-weighted mutual funds (remember, since these are mutual funds, they do not have some of the tax advantages of ETFs—for nontaxable accounts, of course, this should not present an issue), it will also cover equally weighted and value-oriented ETFs.

ACKNOWLEDGMENTS

I am grateful to the many friends, colleagues, and family who have contributed to this project. They, and they alone, are responsible for any errors and omissions found in these pages. Special thanks are owed to Robert Goldstein (my extremely talented partner at Gotham for the last twenty-one years), Richard Greenblatt (my extremely talented brother for the last fifty-plus years), K. Blake Darcy at Gotham Asset Management, Norbert Lou at Punchcard Capital, Edward Ramsden at Caburn Capital, David Rabinowitz at Kirkwood Capital, Adam Barth, Patrick Ede, David Pecora, Yury Kholondyrev, and Kerra Marmelstein at Gotham Asset Management, Linda Greenblatt Gordon at Saddle Rock Partners, John Petry at Columbus Hill Capital Management, Bryan Binder at SAC Capital, Bruce Newberg, Drs. Gary and Sharon Curhan, Michael Gordon at Group Gordon, Allan and Mickey Greenblatt (my wonderful parents), Dr. George and Cecile Teebor (the famous in-laws), Robert Kushel (my broker at Morgan Stanley), Brian Gaines at Springhouse Capital, Rich

Pzena at Pzena Investment Management, Windi Lowell and Bernie Seibert at Gotham Asset Management, and Andrew Tobias.

Thank you to my editor at Random House, Roger Scholl, for all of his encouragement, insight, and patience! Thank you also to my literary agent, Sandra Dijkstra, for her support with this project.

Extra special thanks to my amazing children, Matthew, Rebecca, Melissa, Jonathan, and Jordan—you are my inspiration. Thank you also to my beautiful wife, Julie, for her sage advice with this book, and in life, for her love and support and for each precious day together.